W9-BQK-808

Fallen Soldier

Memoir of a Civil War Casualty

By Andrew Roy

EDITED BY
WILLIAM J. MILLER

MEDICAL COMMENTARY BY
Dr. Clyde B. Kernek

ELLIOTT & CLARK
PUBLISHING

Elliott & Clark Publishing

P.O. Box 551

Montgomery, AL 36101

Copyright © 1996 by Black Belt Communications Group, Inc. Preface, prologue, afterword, and footnotes © 1996 by William J. Miller. Medical commentary © 1996 by Clyde B. Kernek. All rights reserved under International and Pan-American Copyright Conventions. Published in the United States by Elliott & Clark Publishing, a division of the Black Belt Communications Group, Inc., Montgomery, Alabama.

Library of Congress Cataloging-in-Publication Data

Design by Randall Williams

Cover illustration, *1st Minnesota Volunteer Infantry*, by Don Troiani, courtesy of Historical Art Prints, Southbury, Connecticut.

Printed in the United States of America

99 98 97 96   5 4 3 2 1

The Black Belt, defined by its dark, rich soil, stretches across central Alabama. It was the heart of the cotton belt. It was and is a place of great beauty, of extreme wealth and grinding poverty, of pain and joy. Here we take our stand, listening to the past, looking to the future.

Acknowledgments

I must first thank Clyde B. Kernek, M.D., of Carmel, Indiana, for his insightful commentary on the medical aspects of Andrew Roy's fifty-year adventure with a war wound. Dr. Kernek's professional achievements and his love of history give him a unique perspective on the past, and I am grateful he agreed to share that view with readers of this story.

I am grateful as well for the opportunity to thank my friends Robert E. L. Krick and Michael J. Andrus, both historians at Richmond National Battlefield Park and *the* authorities on the Battle of Gaines's Mill, in which Roy fell. Their commitment to their profession inspires me and added materially to this book.

I thank Monica Musick of Manassas, Virginia, who cheerfully and efficiently assisted in preparing the manuscript, Mrs. Frances Hixon, of Jackson, Ohio, who assisted in gathering material on Roy's life in the Buckeye State, and Lisa Cain Curran of Berryville, Virginia, for her help in obtaining photos. The maps were rendered by Terrence Haney of Baltimore, Maryland, who has few peers as a cartographer. My thanks go as well to Carolyn M. Clark, who never fails to recognize a good story, Randall Williams of Montgomery, Alabama, for his his professionalism and cool head under pressure, Jeff Slaton for his careful diligence in helping to bring the many parts of this book together, Steven E. Woodsworth for his clarification of a few of Roy's puzzles, and Mary Ann Harrell and Edwin C. Bearss, who once again made me the beneficiary of their vast knowledge and made this a better book in the process. Finally, as always, I thank my wife, Susan, for all she does and all she is.

Illustrations

Andrew Roy portrait 2

Title Page of the 1909 Edition 8

Map 1, Maryland, Virginia, Pennsylvania, Ohio 15

Map 2, Vicinity of Richmond 18

Map 3, Gaines's Mill Battlefield 20

Private Joseph Stewart 22

Adams House 28

Interior of Libby Prison 51

Janet Watson Roy at age eighteen 82

1907 Surgeon's Certificate 104

Andrew Roy on the occasion of the Lincoln Centennial 116

Contents

Acknowledgments   5

Table of Illustrations   6

Preface   9

Prologue: To the Battle   13

Chapter 1: Wounded   21

Chapter 2: The Humanities of War   27

Chapter 3: A War of Words   31

Chapter 4: Fighting Maggots and Mosquitoes   35

Chapter 5: Hard Times   38

Chapter 6: The Classics   42

Chapter 7: A Change of Base   44

Chapter 8: New Quarters   48

Chapter 9: Heartrending Scenes   52

Chapter 10: Poetry in Prison — Day Dreams   56

Chapter 11: Discussing the Campaign   59

Chapter 12: Paroled   63

Chapter 13: A Visit from the General   66

Chapter 14: Fortress Monroe   69

Chapter 15: The Naval Academy   73

Chapter 16: Clarysville   78

Chapter 17: Surgical Operations   84

Chapter 18: Another Surgical Operation   87

Afterword   91

Medical Commentary on the Case of Andrew Roy   97

Appendix 1: Ordering of Chapters   107

Appendix 2: Roy's Notes on the Pennsylvania Reserves   108

Appendix 3: Roy's Notes on Southern Unionists   110

Appendix 4: Roy's Winter on the Rio Grande   112

Appendix 5: Roy's Recollections of Abraham Lincoln   114

Bibliography   122

Notes   124

Index   153

Recollections *of* A Prisoner *of* War

By ANDREW ROY

SECOND EDITION
REVISED

COLUMBUS, OHIO
J. L. TRAUGER PRINTING CO.
1909

The title page of the 1909 edition of Roy's memoir.

Preface

On Christmas Day 1862, a weary General Robert E. Lee wrote sadly to his wife, "What a cruel thing is war: to separate and destroy families and friends, and mar the purest joys and happiness God has granted us in this world; to fill our hearts with hatred instead of love for our neighbors, and to devastate the fair face of this beautiful world."

Americans are fortunate, perhaps more than they know, that Lee's generation was the last to truly feel the hard hand of war. Except for small wars in our colonial era, the brief four years of domestic strife in the 1860s and the far-flung Indian Wars of the late eighteenth and nineteenth centuries, the United States has been spared the agony of serving as a battleground.

Our insulation from war's hardships, however, can be as much a curse as it is a great blessing. Historians write of "heavy casualties" in battles and tell us how many men were killed and how many wounded. Too often they rely on numbers to portray the extent of suffering. But these words and numbers from the lexicon of carnage mean little to us, for we don't speak the dialect. For them to have any meaning for us, multi-digit casualty figures must be translated into a language we can comprehend.

General Lee's generation needed no such translation. The people of the final forty years or so of the nineteenth century knew about the horror of the battlefield and about the anguish of survival; they felt the ache of loss, the pain of wounds, the pangs of poverty and the hardship of beginning anew. Combat in the Civil War killed or wounded about 710,000 Northern and Southern men in four years — more than 15 percent of the white male population of military age.

Almost one in five soldiers was wounded but, though scarred and perhaps maimed, continued life, at least for a while. This is the story of one of them: Private Andrew Roy of Maryland.

Roy was no better or worse a soldier than millions of other privates North or South, but he was exceptional in that when he sat down to write his memoirs after the war, as many veterans did, he wrote not about the battles, marches and encampments but about his life *after* a bullet hit him in the groin on a summer twilight in 1862.

Roy's memoir is remarkable for its powerful portrait of the relationship between medicine and the human spirit. Medical science had not yet emerged from the shadows of the dark ages in the 1860s. Bacteriology was in its infancy. Surgeons in the Civil War were indifferently trained by contemporary standards; not all of them had what we of the twentieth century would call a medical degree. Staples of modern medicine, like antiseptics and antibiotics, were unknown, and infections were so common that some doctors welcomed them as a beneficial part of the healing process. That the best surgeons of the Civil War era practiced primitive medicine by modern standards is irrelevant. Roy saw two of the best surgeons in the eastern United States, and they operated upon him with "state-of-the-art" technology, which included probing with unsterilized fingers into the patient's abdomen without even local anesthetic. While the surgical technique of the doctors who operated on Roy in 1862 and 1863 falls short of modern standards, we must remember that those professionals were performing to the highest standards of the time. That we know what they did not — about bacteriology, for example — is our advantage, not their shortcoming.

Somehow Roy survived his hideous wound despite receiving almost no medical attention for more than a month after falling on the battlefield. How he endured is a story of dogged personal perseverance. Roy's narrative makes plain how easy it was for many thousands of others to make the journey from the "Wounded" to the adjacent "Killed" column of statistical abstracts. Roy saw men make that transition and suggests that it was occasioned less by carnage wrought upon their anatomy than upon their spirit. For Roy, death was a surrender of the will to live, and, though sorely tested on several occasions, Andrew Roy lived simply because he refused to die.

This book is not so much the memoir of a Yankee private wounded in the Battle of Gaines's Mill as the story of a generation. American farms and factories and shops in the decades after the Civil War were populated by human wreckage — amputees, the deaf and blind, the lame, the disfigured, the dyspeptic, the tubercular and scorbutic. Maimed and chronically diseased young men were a fact of life in the 1860s and

1870s. The chief difference between Roy's drama and those of the half million other wounded survivors of Civil War battlefields — North and South — is simply that Roy wrote his story down. He speaks, therefore, not just for himself but for all those men who returned from war physically broken.

If life's greatest struggles are the loneliest ones — the internal contests we fight with ourselves against fear and resignation — then Roy achieved truly monumental triumphs. In addition to rejecting numerous opportunities to die in the first few weeks after he was wounded, Roy battled on after he was cast off by the army in mid-1863 before his wound was healed. Private citizen Roy was forced to pursue a solitary path toward first a cure then a semblance of a normal life. He found work, built a large family, enjoyed a prosperous career, and even founded a town—all despite a hole in his pelvis that permitted him to walk only short distances with a cane. Those Civil War veterans like Roy who triumphed over crippling injuries and disease did so without the blessings of Veterans' Administration hospitalization or physical rehabilitation sessions with expert therapists. Roy, his comrades, and their former enemies struggled alone and victory came to them only through force of will.

Finally, Roy's tale reminds us of elementary truths that are easily misplaced in the study of history amid a sea of numbers, battle books, biographies and campaign studies: The object of war is to inflict human suffering, and the victim's struggle for survival is tedious, painful and lonely.

• • •

BEFORE BEGINNING ANDREW ROY's story, I offer this brief explanation of how I have reorganized it for the modern reader:

Roy could not write authoritatively about the Civil War beyond his own experience in it, but he nevertheless tried. Roy's memoir presented two principal editorial problems. First, he freely repeated hearsay, occasionally speculated about matters he knew little of and attempted to paint a picture of events with a broad brush, which led to inaccuracies. His first chapter, "The Battle," for example, was an attempt to set the scene and explain the circumstances that brought him into collision with a bullet in the forest near Gaines's Mill. Findings by historians after Roy published his book render much of his first chapter incorrect. The "Prologue: To the Battle" that opens this book is my attempt to set the scene more accurately than Roy could. This Prologue uses Roy's first-hand observations as he recorded them in his first chapter and draws from other sources and replaces his "The Battle." A portion of Roy's first chapter appears in appendix 2.

The second editorial problem might be described as an embarrass-ment of riches. Roy wrote well and was an admirable storyteller, but, like many good spinners of yarns, he occasionally went too far and indulged in lengthy digressions. In my judgment, these flights along divergent tangents weakened the very compelling main story of his struggle to survive his wounds. For example, three chapters had no bearing on his wounding and imprisonment at all: One included his musings on Union sympathies in the South, a second recounted his observations in a postwar trip to Texas and the third recalled the Lincoln-Douglas debates. I excised these three passages and include them in edited versions in appendices 3, 4 and 5 respectively.

With the exception of revisions to Roy's chapters 1 and 21 (now the prologue and appendix 4 respectively) I have edited his text sparingly and tried to alter only those portions that strayed farthest from the main story. Readers interested in precisely how I have reorganized Roy's memoir should refer to Appendix 1 on page 107. If in editing Roy's prose I removed a comment or a digression from the narrative, I included it in a note. Spelling and punctuation have been made somewhat more consistent with modern style.

WILLIAM J. MILLER

Prologue:

To the Battle

O N A SPRING NIGHT in May 1861, twenty-six-year-old Andrew Roy walked into the darkness of the forest outside his mother's Maryland home and struck north for Pennsylvania. He was bound for the army, and the Roys would have been a rare family if under the circumstances both mother and son had not considered the possibility that they might not see each other again. Thirteen months later, Andrew lay stunned and bleeding in a darkening Virginia forest, close enough to death for doctors to tell him he could not live. Soldier friends wrote letters of condolence to his mother. Mrs. Roy put on mourning for her dead son.

But sandy-haired, gray-eyed Private Roy — Scotsman, coal miner, popular comrade, and lover of literature — had not yet passed to the great beyond. He had made it only as far as Richmond, Virginia, which, for Yankee soldiers in 1862, was purgatory only a bit closer to salvation than damnation. Though he had very nearly found a permanent home beneath a mound of earth and a wooden headboard in Virginia's Chickahominy swamps, Mrs. Roy's son was merely a prisoner of war, albeit a severely wounded one. In the days and months ahead, death would approach several times, but good soldier Roy had saved his best fighting for when he needed it most.

Born at Palace Craig, Lanarkshire, in Scotland's Southern Uplands, Andrew Roy came to America with his mother and siblings in 1850. His father, David, a coal miner in the Scottish hills, had come to Maryland two years earlier to secure a job and find a place for his family to live. The Roys settled in coal-rich Allegany County near the town of Frostburg. Andrew was then sixteen and not until 1865 did the families of Allegany

County gain the benefit of public schools, but somehow Andrew acquired a respectable common education and became a lover of the works of Milton, Shakespeare, Byron and especially, like many Scots, of his countryman Robert Burns. Though his early years would be devoted to hard manual labor, Roy would remain bookish throughout his life.[1]

By the time he came to America, Andrew had already worked in the mines of Scotland for eight years, so, as did most young men in the rugged hill country around Frostburg, Roy went to work in the shafts beneath the Alleghenies. He was not content to spend his days eking out a dusty black existence, however, and after just a few years in Frostburg he went west to embrace America's opportunity. He mined in Kentucky and Illinois before landing in Arkansas, where, though only in his mid-twenties, he managed to buy forty acres in the Ozark coal country. He must have considered himself well fixed for a young man and planned to capitalize on the blanket of semi-anthracite coal just four feet beneath the surface of his land.[2]

Unfortunately, Roy's ambitious strides toward peaceful prosperity, like those of millions of Americans, stumbled to a halt in April 1861. After seven Southern states had seceded from the Union and Southerners had fired on Fort Sumter in Charleston Harbor, South Carolina, President Abraham Lincoln called for seventy-five thousand men from the loyal states to suppress the rebellion. Roy left Arkansas hastily and returned to his mother's home in the mountains of the borderland just a few miles from both secessionist Virginia and loyal Pennsylvania.

As a Marylander and an immigrant, Roy might have turned north or south as he stood outside his mother's house that May night. The people of Allegany County among whom Roy had lived had no love of Abraham Lincoln and his ideas — they had given him only one in every seven of their votes in the election of 1860. Nevertheless, Roy seems not to have hesitated. He believed in the union of his adopted country and sought a regiment of loyalists in Pennsylvania. By his own account, he walked twenty-five miles before finding an outfit to sign on with.[3]

By late May 1861, Pennsylvania had already raised more than twenty-five regiments — approximately twenty-five thousand men — in response to Lincoln's call. The Federal war department, conscious of the tremendous expense of keeping regiments armed and equipped, notified the governors of Northern states that no more regiments would be

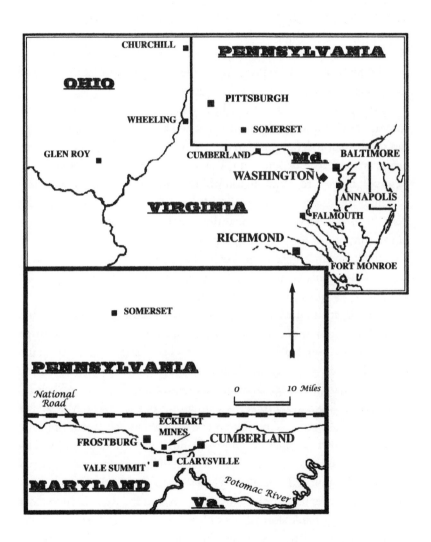

Map 1, Maryland, Virginia, Pennsylvania and Ohio, 1861-1862

accepted. Pennsylvania's governor, Andrew Gregg Curtin, suspected that the war department had been too hasty in denying more recruits and, with the assistance of the state legislature, created a special Pennsylvania Reserve Corps of fifteen thousand men armed and equipped at state expense to defend the Commonwealth against invaders. It was with a company of men destined for the Pennsylvania Reserves that Andrew Roy enlisted somewhere in Somerset County, Pennyslvania. The new recruits made their way to Pittsburgh, where they became Company F of the Tenth Regiment, Pennsylvania Reserve Corps.[4]

Roy spent June and most of July near Pittsburgh learning with his comrades to be a soldier. When the Federal army at Washington sallied toward the Confederates at Manassas, Virginia, in late July and met with defeat at the Battle of Bull Run, Roy and the rest of the Pennsylvania Reserves moved to Washington to reinforce the capital's defenses. Through the rest of the summer and the ensuing winter, Roy and the Pennsylvania Reserves bided their time, marching, drilling and training in preparation for a spring campaign in 1862.[5]

In mid-March began the Peninsula Campaign, the North's first large, well-organized attempt to capture the Confederate capital of Richmond, Virginia. Most of the army moved by steamer down the Potomac River and the Chesapeake Bay to the Virginia peninsula formed by the York and James Rivers. Army commander Major General George B. McClellan intended to move by land and river sixty-odd miles up the peninsula from the Bay to Richmond. The Pennsylvania Reserves, commanded by Brigadier General George A. McCall, remained behind in northern Virginia to protect Washington.[6] In early May, McCall led his men to Falmouth, Virginia, on the Rappahannock River, opposite Fredericksburg, but remained only until mid-June, when the war department sent them to reinforce McClellan.[7] The commanding general immediately attached the Pennsylvanians to the Fifth Corps, commanded by General Fitz John Porter. Porter sent the Reserves to bolster the army's right flank along Beaver Dam Creek, east of Mechanicsville.

Roy and his mates passed the time on Beaver Dam Creek digging entrenchments with picks and shovels and simmering in the humid heat of the Chickahominy swamps.[8] Their peaceful, albeit uncomfortable, existence was interrupted on the afternoon of June 26, when the Confederates suddenly attacked.

General Robert E. Lee, in command of the Confederate army at Richmond for just twenty-five days, had organized a secret offensive and lashed out at McClellan's army in the hope of relieving Federal pressure on the Confederate capital. Lee massed two-thirds of his army for attacks north of the Chickahominy River. The first troops in the path of Lee's juggernaut were the Pennsylvania Reserves at Beaver Dam Creek.

"The weather was hot and dry," Roy recalled, "and we could see by the clouds of dust that the Rebels were advancing to give battle." The Reserves had a very strong position and had strengthened it even more with picks, shovels and axes. Lee's men had little chance in frontal assaults against the muskets and artillery of the well-protected Pennsylvanians. Companies A and B of the Tenth Pennsylvania Reserves fought near Ellerson's Mill on the south-central portion of the Federal line while Roy's Company F and the rest of the regiment remained in reserve, supporting a battery of artillery as interested spectators to the battle.[9] "While the attacking column was crossing a swamp on the double quick, within a hundred yards of the battery," remembered Roy, "it opened on the charging column with grape and canister. The enemy was thrown into confusion and fled." Roy credited the Southerners with bravery in their attacks through the afternoon, "assaulting first one position, then another, in the hope of breaking our lines; but they were repulsed at all points, until darkness closed the combat. They then withdrew out of reach of our fire. During the night some of the wounded made piteous appeals to our men to carry them within the lines and give them water. Our boys would gladly have done so; but were afraid of being fired on in the darkness by the enemy."[10]

The victory at Beaver Dam Creek bore bitter fruit for the men of McCall's ranks. "The boys, who were greatly elated at the outcome of the battle, expected the fighting to be renewed on the following morning," wrote Roy, "and that they would be in Richmond before night. But when morning came we were ordered to fall back to Gaines's Mill, six miles down the Chickahominy. When the boys were ordered to fall back they could not understand what it meant. They had repulsed the enemy at all points, and now were retreating before him." Though his men had held firm and repulsed the attacks, McClellan's position at Beaver Dam Creek had been outflanked by a column under Confederate Major General Thomas J. "Stonewall" Jackson. Roy and his comrades could not then

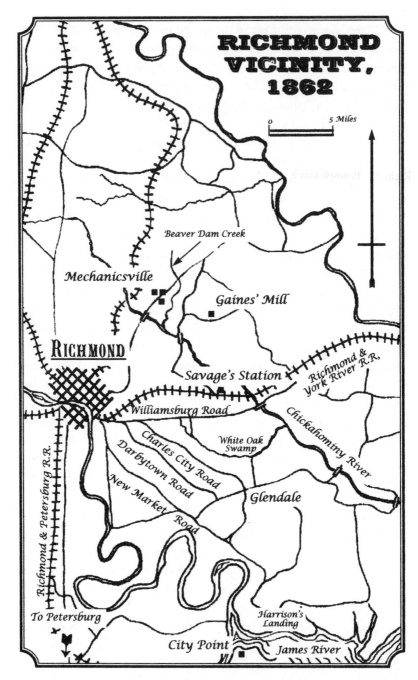

Map 2, Vicinity of Richmond

understand that McClellan had no choice but to withdraw.

Lee's Confederates pursued the retreating Federals past Dr. Gaines's mill and to a strong position east of Boatswain's Creek. Confederates under General A. P. Hill attacked around 2:00 P.M., but made no headway against the Federals behind breastworks in the woods on the slopes of Turkey Hill. Late in the day, Lee, reinforced by about twenty thousand men, launched a general assault against the entire Federal line. The Union line began to crack. "The Rebels hurled column after column upon our lines and forced them, by their superior numbers, to give ground again," remembered Roy. Federal commanders responded to the crisis by sending individual regiments and even portions of regiments to reinforce threatened points. Thus Roy went forward with his company to shore up the hard-pressed Federal line. "The Tenth had been supporting a battery," he recalled, "but toward evening was moved on the firing line, and as the regiment was in the act of forming on the right, by file into line, Company A commenced firing without orders into the Ninth Pennsylvania Reserves, which was in our front, hotly engaged with the enemy. The officers and a number of the cool privates cried, 'Stop firing — the boys in front are our own men.'"[11]

"After order was restored," Roy wrote, "I looked along the line of our regiment and could see the muskets of the boys trembling. The sight did me a world of good, for I thought I was the only man in the regiment possessed of a feeling of fear."

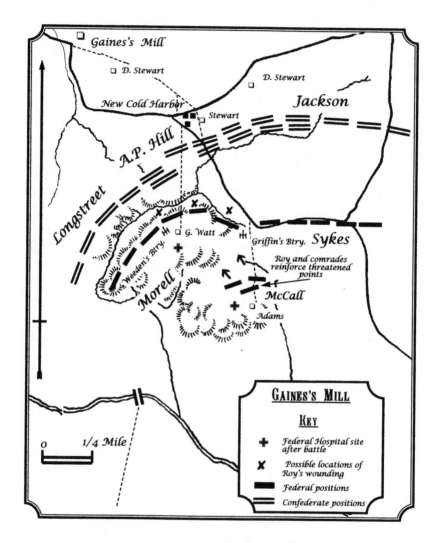

Map 3, Gaines's Mill Battlefield

Chapter 1

Wounded

B EFORE THE TENTH WENT into action, the regiment was ordered to lie down, and when the command was given to charge bayonets they sprang to their feet and made for the enemy. I was in the rear rank, but seeing an opening between Company A and Company F, dashed into the gap. My comrade, on the left, had his hat in his left hand and while waving it aloft and cheering lustily the enemy fired, and he fell dead from a bullet which pierced his heart. At the same moment I felt a terrible blow on the left side, as though some one had struck me with a club, and I was knocked half way round. I leaned upon my musket for support but soon became insensible and fell. When I regained consciousness a comrade was leaning over me; he examined my clothing and found that a minie-ball had passed through my left side, a little above the groin.

The volley which the enemy fired into our charging line, did not even stagger the regiment, and the Rebel line broke and fled pursued by our men. The enemy replaced the gap in their line with fresh troops, who, in turn, forced the boys in blue to give ground. They retired slowly loading and firing. After passing over my body the line halted, and for a few minutes I was lying between the two lines, under a terrific fire from both sides. The Rebels were farthest from me and their balls that fell short, sometimes threw the dirt over my clothes. I expected to be shot again every moment, and was terribly frightened.

It does not require a great amount of courage to go through a battle creditably, for a soldier feels no fear while fighting. It is when he has to take the enemy's fire and cannot return it, that he feels like running away. I, certainly, would have run had I been able. In a few minutes, which I

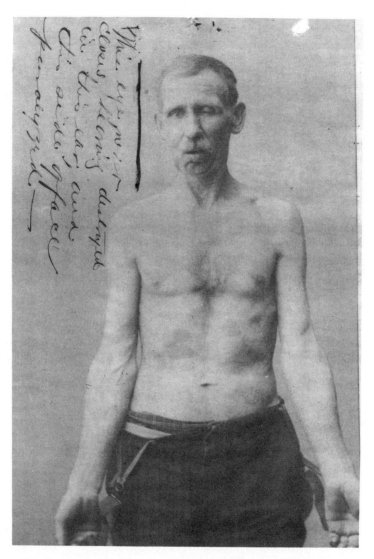

In 1863, Roy served as best man at the wedding of his friend Joseph
Stewart. The two men had served in the same company, were wounded
at about the same time, and left the battlefield in the same ambulance.
This photo, taken about the turn of the century to support Stewart's
claim for a pension increase, shows the damage to his face from the
bullet at Gaines's Mill forty years earlier. The doctor's notes in the
upper left read: "This eye never closes, hearing destroyed in this ear,
and this side of face paralyzed. (National Archives)

thought were hours, the boys in blue went after the boys in gray again with the bayonet, and drove them back to their second line. The hospital corps came with a stretcher, carried me to the rear on their shoulders, and placed me in an ambulance.

It already contained an occupant, a comrade of the same company named Joseph Stewart. He had been shot in the head by a buckshot. This was the second time he had been wounded — the first time on the picket line, six months before — the ball having entered his cheek, passing out through his neck, carrying away part of his jawbone. He had but recently returned to duty when he received the second wound. He had been offered his discharge, but declined to accept it, declaring he would see the end of the war, or leave his bones on the "sacred soil of Virginia."[12]

A few yards from where the ambulance was standing, a battery of six guns was in position. It had no infantry support, they having been transferred to the firing line which the Rebels were making superhuman efforts to break. A Rebel regiment was massing in column of division to charge the battery and soon their yells rose wild and high. Our gunners fired upon them; the driver of the ambulance lashed his horses to a gallop. I turned my head to see the issue of the charge — the gunners were spiking the cannon before abandoning them.[13]

When I was lifted out of the ambulance at the regimental hospital, which was in a hollow, the surgeons were busy with their work of mercy, dressing wounds. Tears were rolling down the cheeks of the assistant surgeon, and the hands and shirt sleeves of both were besmeared with blood.[14] The assistant came over and handed me a bottle of liquor [and] bade me take a good drink; I did so, when he added: "Take more, it will do you good." As soon as he had washed the blood from my wound I inquired if he thought it was fatal; he replied, "It was lucky for you that the ball came out where it did."

It was now sundown; the battle was still raging but the roar of musketry too clearly indicated that our line was giving ground. Shortly after sundown it was broken in the center, but there was no, stampede, for the regulars and zouaves held together and brought up the rear, retiring slowly and in good order.[15] At dark loud shouts were heard in the rear, and were distinctly heard at the regimental hospital where the wounded were lying. The cheering came from General Meagher's Irish brigade, which was advancing as a reinforcement from the other side of the river.[16] But it was too late for further fighting, darkness having thrown her mantle of mercy over the bloodstained field.

About nine o'clock the captain, the first lieutenant and two sergeants came over to the hospital to visit the wounded of the company.[17] After inquiring about my wounds the captain said to me: "Roy, McClellan has taken Richmond."[18]

The captain remained in the hospital until midnight, when he left to take charge of the company, Porter having been ordered by McClellan to withdraw his corps to the south side of the Chickahominy. Before he left I overheard the captain say to the surgeon: — "What a pity for one so young to die so far from home and friends."

"Captain," said I,

> Had I as many lives as I have hairs
> I could not wish them to a fairer death.[19]

Two days later the captain himself was shot through the body in the fourth battle of the Seven Days' Fight and left on the field for dead. One of the boys of the company remained with him, and nursed him back to life. Both fell into the hands of the enemy, and were sent to Richmond. In spite of his cruel wound and lack of proper treatment, the captain recovered, but was not able to longer serve his country. Could he have been spared to the army he would have risen to high command. He had been thirteen months at West Point before the war, and had drilled his company so thoroughly that it looked like regulars on the march or drill.[20]

All the wounded who were able to walk went with their commands to Savage's Station, on the opposite side of the river. Numbers of others were taken across in ambulances. The two sergeants of the company remained with me all night. They had endeavored to secure an ambulance to convey me across the Chickahominy and, failing to get one, offered to carry me across in a blanket, but I was suffering so much that I was unable to stand the trip.

At daybreak the following morning the sergeants made a fire, and were boiling coffee for breakfast, when they observed a cloud of dust indicating the approach of the Confederates. They bolted for the woods and escaped being captured, having gone but a minute when a Confederate vidette rode forward, with a navy revolver in his hand, and asked if we were wounded.[21] On being answered in the affirmative, he replied, "Well, you deserve it for invading our country." I asked him if he knew where our army was; he answered, "It is whipped all to hell."

Said I, "That is not my information; I understand McClellan has taken Richmond."

He threw himself back in his saddle and roared with laughter, exclaiming, "McClellan is killed." I told him I did not believe it.

"Well, he has had an arm shot off," and away he rode, holding his revolver at arm's length.

My wound had pained me so severely all night that at times I could scarcely endure the agony it caused me; but toward daybreak the pain subsided and I was resting easy when the vidette rode up to us.

All the wounded had left, except seven or eight, two of whom had died during the night. These two comrades suffered terribly, and uttered loud lamentations and groans until death kindly stepped in and relieved them of their sufferings. One of the wounded, M. C. Lowry, of Company A, had received a flesh wound in the thigh. He had walked to the hospital after being shot; but the wounded limb afterward became so stiff and sore that he could not accompany the retreating column, and was made a prisoner in the morning. He had been a silent listener to the conversation with the Rebel vidette, and complimented me. He crawled on his hands and one leg to the edge of the woods and, procuring a stout stick, limped back to the fire, which the two sergeants had built, and made some coffee for himself and associates.

This man proved to be my guardian angel; but for his careful nursing I must have died. After partaking of a frugal breakfast of coffee and hard tack we entered into conversation, and I found him very intelligent. He was a school teacher by profession, and had been a reader of books. His home was in Somerset, Pennsylvania.[22]

In the hurry of the retreat one of the hospital corps left his knapsack. It had been placed under my head, and I held on to it. It contained a blanket, a band belt, pen, paper, and ink, and a bundle of letters, all of which I kept, except the letters, which I burned, as they had been written for no other eyes than his.[23] We had unslung our knapsacks, haversacks, and canteens before going into battle, and the knapsack which I "captured" proved a special providence for me.

I had noted down in a memorandum book a synopsis of each day's doings, and as it was in my knapsack I lost it. Some Confederate soldier "captured" it and no doubt keeps it as a war relic.

Chapter 2

The Humanities of War

FITZ JOHN PORTER HAD no sooner crossed the Chickahominy river with his retreating forces than he burned the bridges to prevent Stonewall Jackson from following in immediate pursuit. It took two days to rebuild these bridges, during which time the bulk of the Rebel troops, which had fought at Gaines's Mill, were bivouacked on the field. Jackson detailed a corps of men to gather together the wounded Federal prisoners. About ten o'clock of the forenoon of the day after the battle Confederate privates carried the wounded on stretchers to a mansion which had been a hospital for our sick before the fighting opened. As they laid me on the ground one of them remarked: "This is the gamest Yankee that we have handled today." When they lifted me on the stretcher, seeing that I was very severely wounded, they handled me with great care and did not hurt me, so I replied: "If I have not complained it is due to your care and tenderness, and I thank you for it."

The house was full to overflowing with sick and wounded, and I was placed on the ground, under the shade of a large tree, which served as my quarters for the next two weeks. There were a number of large trees around the house, under whose protecting shade about one-half of the prisoners found rest and shelter from the blazing midsummer sun, until they were removed to the tobacco warehouse in Richmond.[24] All the outhouses, fences, and part of the weather-boarding of the mansion had been used for firewood by our army. The owner of the plantation had removed his family to Richmond on the approach of the Yankees.

He returned, a day or two after the fight, and mixed freely with the wounded prisoners. He told us that he did not know his own farm, so greatly had war's wide desolation deformed it. The most painful incident

The Adams House on the battlefield at Gaines's Mill was a haven for hundreds of wounded soldiers. The injured men lay in and around the house, wherever they could find shelter from the summer sun and rain. Roy was wounded perhaps a half mile from this building, and though he did not precisely identify the building near which he later lay for sixteen days, the scarcity of homes in the area suggests that this might be the house. This 1880s view shows Mrs. Adams on the porch. (U.S. Army Military History Institute)

of his visit, he said, was the loss of a small Shetland pony, which belonged to his little boy. Since removing his family to Richmond, the little fellow had asked his father many times a day, when he was going to get his pony again. Now it was gone and the father hated so badly to go back and tell the boy that the pony had been stolen by the Yankees. The news would almost break his heart. The planter was a man of splendid physique, and was very much of a gentleman. He had no word of complaint to utter, treated the wounded with great courtesy, and recognized the fact that ruin followed on the trail of an invading army.[25]

Jackson detailed a number of Confederate surgeons to care for the wounded prisoners; this being a customary humanity of war. A young doctor approached me and asked to see my wound. He was dressed in a blue uniform and I mistook him for one of our own surgeons, and asked if he were a Federal surgeon. "Sir," he replied, snappishly, "do you mean to insult me?" "No, sir," I retorted, "I meant to honor you." After he had washed the blood off both sides of the wound, I asked him what he thought of my chances of recovery. "Sir, you cannot live three days," was his reply, delivered in a blunt and unsympathetic voice. It is strange, but true, in all wars, that the noncombatants are overcome with war rage, while the soldiers who have met in battle have little feeling against each other.

Surgical science was not as far advanced during the Civil War as it is now, and this was not the only case of a surgeon being mistaken when he told a wounded soldier that he could not live.

A rude operating table was constructed and placed in the shade of a tree, and the surgeons addressed themselves to the work of amputation. More regulars than volunteers, in proportion to their number, were wounded in the limbs, and suffered the loss of a leg or arm.[26] All the patients were put under the influence of chloroform, but a number of them regained consciousness during the operation, and swore worse than the British army did in Flanders, as they writhed in their agony.[27] The surgeons were with us for two days at the plantation house. After treating all the wounded they rolled up their instruments and started out to renew their labors of mercy at some other hospital on the battle-field. We were left without bandages, simplex cerate, or any other necessary articles for dressing our wounds.[28] We were also without medicine for the treatment of the sick.

Jackson, however, detailed six unwounded prisoners to act as cooks and nurses. These poor fellows had more than they could do for the first week, to furnish water to cool our fevered wounds and quench our thirst. There was a fine spring of clear, cold water about fifty yards from the hospital. The nurses carried this water in canteens to the wounded. One of the nurses was a choleric Frenchman, who had seen service under Napoleon the Third.[29] He was very industrious — running to the spring with a load of canteens. As he returned each trip a score of empty canteens would be raised at arms length, their owners yelling at the top of their voices: "Frenchy, Frenchy, fill my canteen." The little Frenchman's vocabulary of English was rather limited, and when his temper got the better of his big heart, he would relieve his surcharged feelings in French, gesticulating and talking twice as fast as an American could. Some of his sentiments would not do to translate and print.

I had become so weak from loss of blood that, when I was raised to a sitting posture to have my wound dressed, I became stone blind. The terrible pain which I at first experienced had, however, subsided, and I could converse freely. Quite a number of the citizens of Richmond had ridden out to the battle field, and were mingling with the prisoners. One of them, noticing that the flies were swarming around my wound, cut a leafy switch from the tree overhead and, sitting down beside me, brushed them away. He chatted with me in a kind and friendly manner, inquired about my home and my friends, and when he left handed me the switch and urged me to use it constantly.

Chapter 3

A War of Words

ON SUNDAY, June 29, Stonewall Jackson rode in camp, and I got a good look at the already famous Confederate general. He was resting on his horse, leaning sideways on his saddle, with one foot out of the stirrup. He was not a man of distinguished appearance. His gray uniform was covered with dust, and he seemed to have a tired, dreamy, far-away look, reminding one of some well-to-do farmer.[30]

Many of the rank and file of Jackson's army, while awaiting the rebuilding of the bridges across the Chickahominy, mingled with the wounded prisoners, and discussed with them the causes and the probable result of the war. Some of them were bitter and defiant in statement, declaring that every man, woman and child in the South would die in the last ditch sooner than submit to subjugation. Quite a number of the privates, and particularly the non-commissioned officers, were men of good social standing, and were well educated. These men laid the blame on such men as Charles Sumner, Horace Greeley and William Lloyd Garrison, as the cause of the war.[31] The majority of the privates, however were of the class known as the poor whites of the South. Few of this constituency could read and write intelligently; but they were as ready with argument as with their muskets to defend their positions; they were, however, better fighters than debaters. They spoke with the accent of the darkeys of the Southern plantations. None of them had ever read a line of the Constitution, but they were ever appealing to it in proof of the justness of their cause.

One of the privates of this class and I held a very friendly conversation on the war question. He belonged to an Alabama regiment, and was barefooted. Before leaving he asked me if I had anything to eat; I answered that I had not; whereupon he thrust his hand in his haversack and taking out a large hard-tack cracker, broke it in two and tendered me one of the pieces, stating it was all he had. I thanked him kindly, but declined the friendly offering, telling him that I could not eat, and that we would be furnished rations by the commissary; he still insisted, but I finally induced him to put it back in his haversack. My shoes were lying beside me and I tendered them to him, but he at first refused to accept them; I urged him to take them; stating that I had no use for them, and would get another pair long before I would be well enough to wear them. He finally consented to take them as a present from me. Having tried them on and finding that they fitted him, he thanked me from the bottom of his heart and went on his way rejoicing. I have always regretted that I did not ask his name and home address, as I would have gladly renewed his acquaintance after the war, in case he survived it. Scenes like these leave an indelible impression on the mind.

M. C. Lowry and I were the only two members of the Tenth Pennsylvania Reserves located at this hospital. We were both laid under the shade of the same tree. He was much less severely wounded, and was much stronger than I. He was intensely patriotic, and neither wounds nor privations could make any impression on his dauntless heart. He engaged earnestly in discussing the issues of the war with the more intelligent Southern soldiers; told them frankly but kindly that the war would never cease until all the seceded states returned to their allegiance to the general government.

Hearing one of our boys say to a Rebel soldier that the war was now practically over; that if the government did not put a stop to it the people would rise up in their might and stop it themselves, Lowry roared at him in rising anger: "You're a damned liar." "There," exclaimed the Southern soldier, "There is a brave man — there is a man who is not afraid to speak his mind."

On another occasion, having got into a discussion with a citizen of Richmond, evidently a man of some consequence in the city, about the relative social status and intelligence of the people of the North and South, the citizen said, among other things, that a Southern man knew more about Chesterfield in five minutes than your Northern mudsill did in a lifetime.[32] Lowry's eyes flashed fire as he retorted: "I have not found all Southerners gentlemen and I'm damned if I am talking to a gentleman now." The boasting son of the South collapsed.

The three days of grace which the Rebel surgeon had informed me would be my allotted span of life having expired, and feeling very weak, although not quite ready to yield up the ghost, I scrawled a brief note to my mother, informing her that I had been very severely wounded in the battle of Gaines's Mill three days before and was a prisoner, with many other wounded men; that my wound was probably fatal, and that as I had no way of sending the letter through the lines, I would put it in my blouse, and if I died the soldiers who buried me would find it in my pocket and mail it as soon as they could. Two comrades of the company I belonged to, however, had written and informed her that her son had been mortally wounded and left with the enemy. Two days later one of the comrades, Thomas Hawley, was himself killed, struck by a cannon ball which carried away one of his legs, at the battle of Glendale. The other, Hugh McMillan, was killed at the second battle of Bull Run, the following August.[33]

The following is a copy of the letter as I remember it:

Gaines Mill, Va., June 30, 1862.

Mrs. Mary Roy,
Frostburg, Aleghany Co., Md.

My Dear Mother — Three days ago I was wounded in the left side, the ball passing through my body just above the groin, in a bayonet charge at the battle of Gaines's Mill, and the wound is probably mortal.

I am a prisoner of war, and am left with many others on the battle-field. I will keep this letter in my blouse pocket, and if I die it will be sent you by some of my comrades after they are exchanged.

Dear mother, farewell.

Your loving son,

Andrew Roy

In a day or two after penning the note to my mother I began to gain strength, and the day before the prisoners were transferred to Richmond, tore it up. On receiving my comrades' letter, mother put on mourning, and was wearing it when I wrote to her, after being paroled, that I was back in "God's country" once more.

The six nurses, and the less severely wounded who were able to assist them, had more than they could attend to, ministering to the sick and helplessly wounded. As soon as I had recovered a little strength, I crawled to the spring to fill my canteen. Having no trousers, I wrapped my blanket around my body as a Scottish Highlander wears his kilt, and fastened it to my waist with the yellow band belt. Having no shirt, I buttoned up my blouse.[34] Notwithstanding these precautions the mosquitoes would find a bare spot and plunge their lances in it.

Chapter 4

Fighting Maggots and Mosquitoes

BEING STILL TOO weak from suffering and loss of blood to fight the flies that swarmed around my wound, it became filled with maggots, as the Richmond citizen predicted it would, in case I did not keep them away with the switch he gave me. Every one of the severely wounded became afflicted equally with myself, with these pestiferous vermin. My friend, Lowry, whose wound was a flesh one, fought the flies away and was not a victim of maggots. He addressed himself to the task of cleaning them out of my wound. He whittled down a short stick to a point, procured a leaf from the tree overhead, and with those rude surgical instruments attacked the enemy. He used the stick to pull out the vermin, holding the leaf under the wound to catch and throw them away.

Lowry made daily attacks, and soon gained ground, but was not able to clean them all out. The wound was about six or seven inches long, and although he attacked the maggots from front and rear alternately, he could not reach the enemy's center. He was a good singer, and while digging deep into the wound with his stick, sang the beautiful song of "Annie Laurie," which every soldier knew by heart, and which on the march the whole army would often sing with such volume of voice that it could be heard several miles distant. While Lowry was chanting the song his eye had a dreamy look, for his mind was back in the hills of his native state, where "the girl he left behind" lived and loved him; and it revived many memories of the land of my birth and boyhood. I copy the song from memory:

Maxwellton braes are bonnie,
  Where early fa's the dew;
'Twas there that Annie Laurie
  Gaed me her promise true:
Gaed me her promise true,
  Which ne'er forgot shall be;
And for bonnie Annie Laurie
  I'd lay me doon and dee.

Her brow is like the snaw-drift
  Her throat is like the swan:
Her face it is the fairest
  That e'er the sun shone on —
That e'er the sun shone on.
  And dark-blue is her e'e:
And for bonnie Annie Laurie
  I'd lay me doon and dee.

Like dew on the gowan lying
  Is the fa' of her fairy feet:
And like simmer soft winds sighing,
  Her voice is low and sweet —
Her voice is low and sweet.
  And she's a' the world to me:
And for bonnie Annie Laurie
  I'd lay me doon and dee. [35]

One poor fellow, who lay next to me, had been wounded in the neck and was literally covered with maggots. When the nurses lifted him to a sitting position to dress his wound, the sight was heart-rending. He could not speak, being too far gone for utterance, and died the following day.

The Richmond government, as soon as it was informed of the condition of our wounded, sent out a supply of turpentine to our nurses, which they poured into our wounds. The maggots now bit harder than ever. It now a question for some hours whether they would kill the wounded or the turpentine would kill the maggots. The endurance of the soldiers triumphed, and we were not further troubled with the pestiferous vermin.[36]

But we still had another enemy to meet, the mosquitoes. They bit harder than any mosquitoes that I have ever seen, before or since. Every time they inserted their long, sharp bills into our poor bodies they drew blood. We fought them off with some degree of success during the day, but while asleep at night we were at their mercy, and they were strangers to mercy. We were awakened again and again by the pain of their merciless lances, and in the morning our faces looked in many cases as though we had been in a prize fight.

Many melancholy scenes were witnessed during our sixteen days' sojourn on the battle field. Among the more very severely wounded was a tall boy, evidently not more than sixteen years of age. He was shot in the back, and the wound paralyzed both of his legs. He had been laid down in the shade of the planter's house; as the day advanced the shade left him, and he was exposed to the fierce rays of a midsummer sun. He would then call piteously for somebody to move him over into the shade, and if his call was not immediately answered would burst out in loud lamentation. One of the wounded, a regular, whose arm had been shot away in battle, went over to him and told him that if he did not cease crying he would horsewhip him. "I am wounded," moaned the poor boy. "So are we all wounded; but that is no excuse for a soldier playing the baby," cried the one-armed soldier.

Men died every day from the severity of their wounds; or from lack of medical treatment. The nurses carried the dead out about twenty or thirty steps from the camp and threw a few shovelfuls of dirt over the bodies. The rain cracked the thin covering of earth, exposing the bodies which had become a mass of maggots. General Sherman never said a truer thing than, "War is Hell."[37]

Among the slightly wounded was a tall and handsome man about thirty years of age. He had been wounded in the knee and ought to have gotten well soon; he had a wife and family whom he dearly loved. He fretted so much about them that it made him sick. He would often say, "Oh, if I could only send word to my wife and children what a load it would take off my mind;" then he would ask the comrades, "Do you think we will ever get out of this place?" I endeavored to comfort the poor fellow by telling him that wars always produce similar suffering and privation, and hoped that we would live to tell our friends the thrilling story of our prison life.

Chapter 5

Hard Times

AFTER STONEWALL Jackson's command left to join their comrades in pursuit of McClellan's retreating army and the Richmond citizens had become tired of visiting the battlefield and looking at the wounded Yankee prisoners, we were left alone in our misery.[38] The more slightly wounded were becoming able to hobble to the spring for water to dress their wounds and quench their thirst. All the prisoners except the incurably wounded became more cheerful and lighthearted as their strength began to come back to them.

Occasionally some convalescent Confederate soldier would pass en route to join his regiment, and leave a copy of a Richmond paper, which we eagerly devoured, for we possessed no means of getting news about our own army, nor of sending communications through the Rebel lines, and anything in the line of a newspaper was "a welcome visitor to our home circle." The Confederate papers were full of the most absurd accounts of the series of battles which occurred during the six days of McClellan's retreat, and predicted that the Yankee government would *soon* acknowledge the independence of the Southern Confederacy.

I had lost my cap while being lifted into the ambulance; had given my shoes to a kind-hearted Confederate soldier who was bare-footed; had my pants taken off when my wound became filled with maggots, and a straggling Johnny Reb stole them; had torn up my shirt for bandages; and all my worldly possessions in the way of clothing consisted of my blouse, a pair of socks, and a blanket — the latter I found in the knapsack which I had picked up at the regimental hospital the day after the battle of Gaines Mill, but,

Man wants but little here below,
Nor wants that little long. [39]

I wrapped my body in the blanket, kept my blouse buttoned up to protect myself from the lances of the mosquitoes, and having regained a little strength, fought off the flies as best I could with a leafy switch; poured cold water on my wound which cooled the fever and kept down the inflammation; and was not altogether unhappy. Lying under the shelter of a friendly tree, I breathed the pure, sweet air of heaven, and heard the sweet songs of birds.

There were several heavy rains the first week of our imprisonment. During the storm I took refuge in the planter's house.[40] It[41] was so full of wounded men that the air was foul from the emanations of their lungs and wounds, and I was glad to get back under the tree again as soon as the rain was over. Many of the wounded preferred to bide the pelting of the pitiless storm[42] to the sickening stench of the house. Their frames had become so toughened by exposure in the bivouac and on the march that a shower of rain had no terror for them. When the sun came out, their clothes soon dried on their backs.

Depressing as the situation was, there was not a single regret expressed by any of the wounded that they had enlisted to fight for the preservation of the Union. All were ready as soon as their wounds were healed, to return to duty and assist in the overthrow of the rebellion, that the government, bequeathed by their fathers, might be handed down unimpaired to their children.

After we had been nine days on the battlefield everything in the commissary had been eaten up. The conviction forced itself upon us that the Rebel government had deliberately determined to let us die of starvation; and curses both loud and deep were heaped upon Jeff. Davis and his despicable Confederacy. We reasoned that a government which would allow wounded prisoners of war to remain on the battlefield without shelter, or medicines, or medical attendants, was heartless enough to abandon them to die of starvation.[43]

In the hasty retreat of our troops across the Chickahominy, the commissary department had thrown out some wagon loads of hardtack near where we lay; but the recent rains had reduced the whole of it to a pulpy mass, bespattered with mud.[44] The nurses and the wounded who could walk went after this dirty paste, selected the best of it, and brought it to their helpless comrades, and for two days this was the only food we had. Sharing the general feeling that we had been abandoned to perish of starvation, I penned a vigorous letter to one of the Richmond papers, protesting against such inhuman treatment, and closed the communication with the statement that "the brave but unfortunate prisoners knew how to die for the Union."[45]

I read the letter to two of my comrades, Lowry and Sayers, for their opinion of its propriety. Both heartily approved of it. Lowry, however, asked me to erase the word "brave," stating that it smacked of boasting; but Sayers stood up for the letter as it was written, and said that if we were to die of starvation it was well to let the Rebel government know that we died game, and Lowry yielded. But before an opportunity offered to send the letter into Richmond, a supply of hard tack was sent out to us.

Lowry was killed at the battle of Fredericksburg the following December; but Sayers survived the war, and is still living. We did not hear from each other for several years after we were paroled, when I received the following letter from him:

Waynesburg, Greene County, Pa.,
July 10, 1866.

Mr. Andrew Roy, Sharon, Pa:

Dear Sir — came across a Scotchman from West Virginia the other day, and in our sociable I told him I would like to know the whereabouts of a countryman of his who served in the Tenth Pennsylvania Reserves, by your name — the man who laid with me on the battlefield of Gaines Mill, a prisoner of war — and I am informed that you are the man. Were you not wounded in the groin, and do you not remember a man of the Eighth Pennsylvania dressing your wound, and assisting or rather partly dictating a letter to the Richmond *Dispatch* about the starvation of our prisoners, when happily hard tack was brought the same evening by the rebels, which we exchanged for flour? We saw Stonewall Jackson Sunday, June 29th.

It was not my suffering with you that made me inquire for you, but your grit, or otherwise true patriotism, though a wounded soldier, in defending the cause of the Union against the rebel soldiers and citizens, who visited the battlefield after the retreat of our army. How have you been prospering since the war? Please answer, and I shall be glad to hear from you.

    Your comrade,

      Robert A. Sayers

Next to Lowry, Sayers was the best friend I had. He was wounded in the thigh and was soon able to limp about with the aid of a sapling of the forest. He was well educated, and was a college student when the war broke out. He brought me water from the spring and dressed my wound. We have met since the war and still correspond.[46]

Chapter 6

The Classics

QUITE A NUMBER of the wounded prisoners were men of superior education, and possessed a taste for the classics. Not having access to books, they whiled away the lazy, leaden-stepping hours rehearsing the works they had read, and had eager listeners. I was fortunately able to quote many passages from Shakespeare, Byron and Burns, also selections from Books V and VI of *Paradise Lost,* which I had memorized while digging coal in the mines of Arkansas the year before the war, and they were still fresh in my memory.[47] These books relate to the Rebellion in Heaven, where Satan, fraught with envy against the Son of God, summoned all his regent powers to give battle to the Almighty, and establish his throne equal to that of the Most High.

Millions of fierce-contending angels fought on either side, who tore the hills from their foundations and hurled them in mid-air against each other's line of battle. Horrible confusion rose, which would have wrecked Heaven itself, had not the Almighty commissioned His Son to go to the front, in his Great Father's Might, armed with his bow and thunder to assume command of the loyal angels. The presence of the Son withered all the strength of Satan and his rebellious crew, who fled like a herd of timorous goats before the victorious army of the Great Son of God, who pursued them:

> With terrors and with furies to the bounds
> And crystal walls of Heaven, which opening wide
> Rolled inward, and a spacious gap disclosed
> Into the wasteful deep.[48]

I have never met an American who was not an admirer of the poetry of Robert Burns. The Boys in Blue were no exception, and I was called upon to recite "Tam O'Shanter," the "Cotter's Saturday Night," and everything else I had memorized of Scotia's darling poet.[49] Passages from Shakespeare, Byron, Longfellow, Bryant and Whittier were read from memory by one or another of the comrades, during the sixteen days we passed together under the open sky.[50]

The prisoners represented five or six different states but the majority of them were from Pennsylvania, New York and Michigan. Quite a number were regulars who represented no state in particular. One of the regulars was an Irishman, who possessed a fund of Irish stories, which he would relate with the vivacity of disposition and gaiety of manner for which the Irish race is generally and justly famed. Although a Catholic, he could crack a joke at the expense of the priest with the zest of a Scotch Presbyterian. One of his stories was about a countryman of his, who was a heavy drinker, but otherwise a fine fellow. He had been induced by a number of friends, who recognized his many good qualities of head and heart, to join the sons of temperance. For some time he held steadfastly by his pledge. At last, however, his old craving for drink got the better of him, and placing an empty glass behind his back, he asked some of the bystanders to put a sup of liquor into it unbeknown to him. Lincoln used to tell this story, locating the scene in Springfield, Ill.

Another story of our friend was that of a man who went to the priest to get his sins forgiven. While confessing the man stole the priest's watch, and holding it up before him, said, "Here is a watch which I have stolen, and I will give it to you." His reverence told the man that he could not accept of stolen goods, and ordered him to go to the owner of the watch and give it back to him; "I have done so," said the man, "and he would not take it from me, and so I offer it to you." "Go back the second time and tender the owner his watch; if he will not take it you may keep it." "I have tendered it to the owner twice, your reverence." "Then," said the priest, "keep it." And the thief went his way rejoicing.

Chapter 7

A Change of Base[51]

FTER THE PRISONERS had been held two weeks on the battlefield, they were notified that they would be transferred to Richmond in a day or two. The news was received with great satisfaction; but little did we think that the change would be worse than jumping out of the frying pan into the fire. By this time those who had received flesh wounds were, in most cases, in a fair way to recovery. Those who had an arm shot away were able to walk about; those who had lost a leg were able to hobble on crutches. Many of the severely wounded had died.

We looked upon the transfer to Richmond to mean that we were about to be either paroled or exchanged; or at worst to have an opportunity of sending letters through the lines to our friends at home, whose anguish touching our fate made many a stout heart sick. We had heard nothing from home, nor of the army, since the campaign opened. How it would gladden the hearts of parents, wives and children, brothers and sisters, to learn that we were alive: who, uncertain of our fate, were like Rachel weeping for her children and would not be comforted.[52]

We were carried in wagons to Savage's Station, seven miles from Gaines's Mill, thence by rail on the Richmond and York railroad.[53] The teams arrived on the fifteenth, but it took two days to complete the transfer to Savage's Station.[54] The road had been built by our army, and consisted of a series of fallen trees laid skin-tight the whole length of the way.[55] The drivers whipped their horses to a trot, and the badly wounded suffered terribly. I was not able to sit up, and lay full length in the bed of the wagon, suffering the most cruel agony from the jolting it made. I appealed to the driver to drive slower, but he paid no attention to the appeal, and seemed to take fiendish delight in the torture he was inflicting. Finding that I could not move his stony heart, I shut my teeth tight and bore without complaint his heartless cruelty.

When we reached Savage's Station I was thoroughly exhausted and lay down to rest. Soon a comrade of the same company, who had been wounded in the same battle, passed by. He expressed great surprise at seeing me, as he understood that I had died the day after the battle and was reported dead in the company. He was wounded in the side and had walked to Savage's Station with the retreating army the night of the battle, but was unable to proceed further and was taken prisoner.

Before the Seven Days fight began, Savage's Station was the site of the General Hospital of McClellan's army. When the campaign opened there were twenty-five hundred sick and wounded in this hospital, most of whom, together with the medical stores, fell into the hands of the enemy. Two days after the battle of Gaines's Mill another battle was fought here, in which our men, although severely pressed by the Rebels, broke their line by a bayonet charge. McClellan's objective was the James River, and he ordered his victorious troops to continue the retreat. Most of the prisoners had been forwarded to the tobacco warehouses in Richmond, or to Belle Isle on the James River, near Richmond, before the contingent arrived from Gaines's Mill.[56]

Savage's Station being on the railroad, the Richmond papers found their way among the prisoners. The account of the campaign which they contained was a monstrous caricature. Our army had been all but annihilated in a series of battles which had been fought during the six days' retreat to the James River, and was cowering under the cover of the gunboats; the South had practically conquered their independence. The doughty editorial warriors of the Sanctum Sanctorum were terrible fighters.[57]

There being no train to convey us to Richmond that day, I was only too glad to pass the night at the Station; for I was tired, sore and sick from the terrible jolting of the wagon over the corduroy road. Here I was furnished with a shirt and shoes, and I bought a pair of army pants with the last five dollar bill that I possessed. After a supper of hard tack and coffee, I dressed my wound and lay down on a cot, under cover of a tent, and slept the sleep of innocent childhood. The next morning I felt all right, the soreness caused by the rough and tumble ride having left me.

About three o'clock in the afternoon the train which was to convey our contingent of prisoners to the Rebel capital came steaming into the station. It consisted of a number of box cars and one regular passenger coach; the box cars being for privates and non-commissioned officers; the coach for the accommodation of the officers. There were points en route to Richmond where pickets were stationed, who cheered in triumph at our expense; perhaps they were home guards; for soldiers who have faced each other in battle seldom exult over a wounded foe.

We were probably two hours in reaching the Rebel capital.[58] As we filed out of the depot and formed in line of march, the sidewalks were filled with people of both sexes, and all ages, to see the Yankee prisoners. We were a heterogenous mass of humanity. All were dirty; many were in rags, some had lost a leg, others an arm, many had wounded arms in a sling, others their heads tied up; all were thin and emaciated from exposure and lack of medical attention and proper food. An important looking citizen on horseback, probably the mayor of the city, cried out to us: "Boys, charge all this up to religious fanaticism."[59]

The Rebel officer gave the command, "Forward, march," and we started along the street with a slow and solemn step to a tobacco warehouse, which had been assigned for our prison quarters. A file of Confederate soldiers were placed on each side of the entrance of the prison to search the prisoners before they entered the building. All found with revolvers and knives were required to hand them over to the guards; but any one who possessed a watch, or money, was allowed to retain it.

I had the yellow regimental band belt around my body; and before reaching the entrance to the prison, a citizen offered me a dollar and a half in Confederate money for it, and I gladly accepted the offer. At this early stage of the war, the Rebel money had not greatly depreciated in value, and I bought bread with it in the prison at ten cents a loaf.

The prisoners filed up the steps to their respective quarters as the guards directed. The building had been used as a prison ever since the first battle of Bull Run, July 21, 1861, and had just been emptied before our arrival, the former occupants having been transferred to Belle Isle on the James River.

Having become worn out, sore and feverish by the march from the depot to the prison, I stretched myself full length on the dirty floor, in anything but a pleasing frame of mind. The lines over the gates of Hell in Dante's Inferno can best express my feelings:

Abandon Hope All Ye Who Enter Here.[60]

Chapter 8

New Quarters

THE TOBACCO warehouse was so crowded with prisoners that there was scarcely room to lie down; and we soon discovered that it was inhabited by another species of animated nature. Next day, for some reason, we were removed to another tobacco warehouse on the same street. There were 805 prisoners confined in this building, which was three stories in height. One hundred and sixty-five occupied the third floor — the room to which I was assigned.[61]

The room was divided up into imaginary sections for bed rooms; two by six feet being allotted to a prisoner. A space two feet wide ran along the whole length of the building between the rows of prisoners — this was a street or passage in which we might walk to and fro. There were several of these streets between the rows of prisoners. A wider passageway ran at right angles to these parallel passage ways, leading to the stairway outside. In the rear of the building there was a large water tank which was filled with water from the canal, and there were several out-houses for the calls of nature.

There was a medical director, several nurses and cooks allotted to each room. The doctor was allowed to go outside for necessary medical supplies. He was a whole-souled, big-hearted man, cheerful of manner and kind of speech; and was universally liked by the prisoners. Some of the nurses, too, were allowed to go out on business connected with their office; they never failed to bring back their canteens filled with clear cold water, which they gave to the badly wounded and dying soldiers.[62]

The floor of the room was covered for several inches with dried and hardened tobacco juice. This was the mattress on which we slept, our covering being the black and dirty ceiling overhead.[63]

The scorching mid-summer sun raised the temperature of the water in the tank to such a degree that it burned our mouths in drinking it. When it rained hard the water became brown as a brick; but we had to drink it or go without. During the whole time of our confinement in the tobacco warehouse many of the prisoners never once enjoyed the luxury of a drink of pure, cold water, and none of them got more than two or three mouthfuls.

Our rations were half a loaf a day — a half ration. I was more fortunate than most of my associates, however, as I bought with my Confederate money, received for my belt, an occasional loaf of bread from vendors,[64] who were permitted to sell to us. There was very little money among the prisoners, as they had not been paid for two months before the fighting began.

We sometimes were treated to half a bowlful of "beef tea," which the boys with perfect truth called dish water. Once I bought a piece of fresh meat, and laid half of it aside for my friend Sayers. He was down in the middle room at the time visiting a comrade. When he returned the meat was fly-blown and he could not eat it.

Comrade Lowry was located on the floor below, and he did not call for a day or two. When he came he said in a serio-comic voice, "Well, Roy, what do you think of our new hotel quarters as compared to the green fields of Gaines's Mill?"

Said I, "Lowry, do you remember Satan's soliloquy, after he recovered from his stupor on being hurled down into the bottomless pit?

> Farewell, happy fields; hail, horrors; hail
> Infernal world; and thou profoundest Hell
> Receive thy new possessor, one who brings
> A mind not to be changed by place or time;
> The mind is its own place and in itself
> Can make a heaven of hell and a hell of heaven.[65]

I wish I had only half of Satan's courage, as Milton portrays it in *Paradise Lost.*

"All right," replied Lowry, "but you must remember that Satan was never confined in a tobacco warehouse, in the Capital of the Southern Confederacy; otherwise he would not have been so courageous and self-contained. Well, we must make the best of it we can for, as Shakespeare says:

> Things are never at worst
> So long as we can say: "This is the worst."[66]

And he left me promising to "call again."

Comrade Campbell, of my own company, was in the third or upper room.[67] He often came over to see me and talk about old times in the regiment, and our quiet and happy homes far away. Sayers was also on the same floor, and we were much together. Campbell had a bad wound; but he was a strongly-built young man, in the first flush of full-grown manhood, and his courage was like his frame.

The accommodations in the back yard providing for the calls of nature were insufficient for the purpose. Occasionally as many as twenty soldiers would be standing in single file awaiting their turn, and when the promptings of nature could no longer be controlled the poor fellows violated the proprieties. Prisoners too sick or badly wounded to crawl to the sinks were frequently found wallowing in their own filth. In later years, when peace had spread her white wings over the land, Comrade Sayers wrote me:

> I distinctly remember the scenes you describe, particularly the letter to the Richmond paper about the starvation of our prisoners; but I do not remember Lowry. He must have been an intimate friend of yours belonging to the same regiment. But the truth is, all the Pennsylvania Reserves were soul and body brothers. They were blood and relations in one sense at least — they bled, suffered and died together on many a hard fought battle field.
>
> Stricken down in the early part of the war, I saw little of the hard fighting, compared to many; but I saw enough of Rebel prison life to appreciate the horrors of those infernal hells, in which studied neglect, for the sole purpose of producing disease and death were daily practiced. Who will forget those scenes of wounded men wallowing helpless in their own filth, covered with vermin, and starved into disease, idiocy and death.
>
> When I think of those days, I wonder how any soldier can be a

Democrat, especially any one who ever experienced the horrors of those infernal dens. If wounds and privations in Rebel prisons will not knock the Democracy out of a man I wonder where the honor and brains of such a man can dwell."[68]

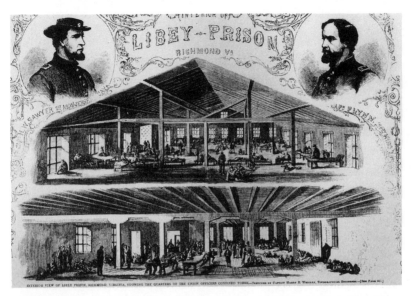

Libby Prison at Twentieth and Cary Streets in Richmond was a former tobacco warehouse adjacent to the Kanawha Canal. Libby became the busiest prison of the war—between March 1862 and April 1865, an estimated 125,000 Federal prisoners spent time there, about a thousand at a time. Libby occasionally housed enlisted men, many, like Roy, wounded in recent battles, but later housed only officers captured by the Confederates. This engraving (which misspells the name of the prison) from a period newspaper was sketched by former prisoner Captain Harry E. Wrigley and depicts the large, barren rooms in which Roy and his comrades endured the heat, filth, and depression of captivity in July 1862. (U.S. Military History Institute)

Chapter 9

Heartrending Scenes

I HAD TWO COMRADES, both terribly wounded, who occupied bedroom space with me on the tobacco stained floor. I occupied the middle of the bed. Both comrades, in addition to their wounds, were burning with fever. The second day they sank rapidly, and in the afternoon they died.

I turned my head to watch them die. They expired within five minutes of each other. Neither of them ever spoke. As soon as the doctor's attention was called to their death, he had the remains removed, and the bedroom space made vacant was filled by other prisoners.

In that closely packed room, where nearly two hundred men were quartered, most of them wounded, the stench which filled the room was suffocating.[69] My lungs soon became so clogged up that I could not breathe without suffering, and I had a pain in my breast all the time I was in the tobacco warehouse. A number of the unwounded would sit on the window sills of the prison, with their legs hanging outward, and nearly filled the space through which the fresh air of Heaven might otherwise have entered the building. This was against the rules, and the Rebel guards in the street would order them back into the room; they, however, would disregard them and return again. In no case which came under my observation did the guards ever raise their pieces on them. It was frequently published in the Northern papers that the Rebel guards had shot some of the prisoners at the windows; but the statement was unwarranted and untrue. The guards were, on the contrary, exceedingly forbearing when their orders were disregarded.[70]

I was able in a day or two to go down the stairway to the water tank in the back yard to dress my wound. On one of these occasions I met the tall New Yorker at the tank dressing his wounded knee. He was not looking well, and was feverish.

"O, Roy," he said, "we will never get out of this horrible place; I will never see my wife and children any more. The settled purpose of the Rebel government is to kill all the prisoners by neglect and starvation. How can a government which pretends to be civilized have the heart to treat its prisoners as we are being treated? O, if I could only see my wife and children again I would not mind it so much."

I promised to call on him, and bade him cheer up; that we would all get home after a while and live and laugh at this hereafter. I visited him the following day and found him stretched full length on the floor with a high fever. Sayers went down to see him later in the day, and on returning said to me: "The New Yorker is a very sick man; I believe he is dying, go down and talk to him." I did so, but he refused to be comforted. He died next day.

The death of this comrade filled my heart with sorrow; for I had become greatly attached to him. I blamed myself for not taking his home address. His poor wife and children would probably never know when and where he died. It would have been a great consolation to them to have been informed that his greatest sorrow, as a prisoner of war, was that he could not communicate with them and send them his love, and to know how often and how lovingly he had spoken of them.

There was not chair nor table to rest on; no needle or thread with which to mend our clothes, not water, soap or towels in the prison. The pale and emaciated condition of the prisoners, the daily deaths, sometimes amounting to a dozen, and the ever increasing number of sick were enough to rend the stoutest heart. We would see from the back windows of the prison the Rebel Capitol, with the Rebel flag waving over it, and curses both loud and deep were freely expressed that Jeff Davis and the flag, too, might be hurled down.

> To bottomless perdition; there to dwell
> In adamantine chains and penal fire.[71]

These were not the words used; my pen is not able to transcribe them, and if it were, they would not look well in print.

Owing to the severity of my wound I was not able to walk, except with suffering, and passed most of the wearisome hours stretched full length on the floor. An occasional newspaper would find its way to the prison, which was read with the greatest eagerness. Frequently, to take my mind off the gloomy and depressing situation, I would watch, timepiece in hand, our hemipterous comrades creeping on the tobacco stained floor — watch them "sprawling and sprattling in shoals and nations," to borrow emphasis from the poetry of Robert Burns.[72] Their maneuvers sometimes reminded me of a line of skirmishers.[73]

To keep these comrades from becoming too familiar with our poor bodies we shed our clothing twice a day, and slew all we would find. This gave us relief for the time being; but notwithstanding our repeated attacks they became more numerous and formidable every day. The red, inflamed spots — and their number was legion — with which our bodies were covered, too palpably demonstrated that if we did not carry on a defensive war we would sooner or later bite the dust ourselves. It was a war of opposing and enduring forces.[74]

In the course of two or three weeks a number of the convalescent prisoners were removed to Belle Isle. This gave us more room in which to walk about the prison, but made little if any difference in its sanitary condition; the vapid atmosphere, the sickening odor, the filthy floor with its thousands of body lice remained. The hand of death also remained.

To escape from the foul and noxious atmosphere of the tobacco warehouse, I frequently rested awhile in the back yard, after dressing my wound. The scorching rays of the mid-summer sun were hard to endure, but were a relief from the horrible stench of the prison. Quite a number of the wounded were not thoughtful in this matter, and died victims to the polluted atmosphere.

My wound continued to discharge pus as copiously as ever, although I was gradually gaining in strength. I made at least a half dozen trips a day to the cistern in the back yard to wash the bandage and dress the wound. I had only one rag — a piece of my shirt, which I had torn up a day or two after the battle of Gaines's Mill, to cover the wound.

There was an abundance of water at all times in the tank, to which we would help ourselves to clean our wounds and wash our bandages.[75] By turning a faucet we got water from the canal to drink, but it required a great exercise of courage, even when choking, to swallow it by reason of its high temperature. We never washed our clothes at all; had we washed them they would have been as dirty as ever the first night, after sleeping on the filthy, tobacco-stained floor.

A number of intelligent Southern soldiers, who were confined in the military prisons of the North during the War of the Rebellion, have done their best to convince themselves and others that the treatment they received was as bad as that of the Northern soldiers confined in Southern prisons. Military prison life is bad enough at best, under the most humane of governments, but there is no comparison between the treatment the prisoners received in the North and in the south. The passions excited by the Civil War have now died out, and there remains nothing of the old bitterness and hatred. The Southern soldiers were utterly brave, and it was an honor to meet such men in battle; but the military prisons of the South were a disgrace to the civilization of the nineteenth century.[76]

Chapter 10

Poetry in Prison — Day Dreams

ONE DAY COMRADE Lowry came to see me with animation in his gait, and a broad smile overspreading his face. He held a newspaper in his hand. "Roy," said he, "this paper contains a poem on Napoleon by Lord Byron. Let us memorize it. It is a magnificent poem and contains eleven stanzas; I have just finished reading it. You can have the paper for an hour, then I will call for it and keep it an hour; we will exchange the paper every hour until we have the poem memorized, and see who comes out victor." I gladly fell in with the idea, mauger the suspicion that I would come out of the contest second best.

I read the poem carefully through, and then commenced to commit it to memory, stanza by stanza. Lowry returned at the expiration of the hour, took the paper, and began to memorize the poem in the same manner. Neither of us reported progress, until Lowry returned before I had quite completed mastering the poem, and said "I have it," at the same time handing me the paper to hold while he recited it. He had the poem memorized word for word, and I acknowledged defeat. I find, after the lapse of forty-two years, that I have forgotten it, with the exception of one or two stanzas. The last one I still remember and transcribe from memory:

> He who ascends to mount tops shall find
> The loftiest peaks most rapt in clouds and snow.
> He who surpasses or subdues mankind
> Must look down on the hate of those below.
> Though high above the sun of glory glow,

And far beneath the earth and ocean spread,
Round him are icy rocks, and loudly blow
Contending tempests on his naked head:
And thus reward the toils that to those summits led.[77]

After the war I came across the same poem in "Childe Harold's Pilgrimage." The poem is complete in itself. Indeed, "Childe Harold's Pilgrimage" is a series of poems strung together. Byron's poem on Waterloo, beginning "There was a sound of revelry by night," which every schoolboy knows by heart, is another poem complete in itself, and has no connection with the "Pilgrimage of Childe Harold," but has a good deal to do with the pilgrimage of Napoleon Bonaparte to the Island of St. Helena.[78]

The mental exercise of memorizing the apostrophe to Napoleon in the Libby prison was a labor of love. I had always been a reader of poetry, and would have given all the money Uncle Sam owed me at the time for three books, namely, Shakespeare, Milton and Burns. But no books being accessible I had passed away many an otherwise weary hour in day dreams, touching the outcome of the War of the Rebellion. I would discuss the question with myself whether or not the Southern people, who are hopelessly in the wrong, will succeed in breaking up the Union. They are terribly earnest in this war. No rebellion of such formidable proportions has ever been put down. Will a just God hearken to the prayers of a people fighting to establish a government, the corner stone of which is founded on human slavery? If the Rebellion is overthrown will the warring sections live in peace and harmony, or will the South at the first favorable opportunity rebel again, as Scotland did under her hero, Sir William Wallace, and her hero king, Robert Bruce?[79] I thought, however, that this reasoning was defective — Scotland fought for liberty from a foreign yoke; the South is fighting for slavery.[80]

"Might," it is said, "makes right, and Providence is on the side of the heaviest battalions."[81] Without the railroads could the rebellion have been put down? I presume these and similar questions were racking the brains of thousands of people at the same time. Happily the Civil War was settled right, never to be renewed.

On the morning of July 21st there was unusual activity manifested in the streets of Richmond. Small boys began bursting firecrackers and the Rebel Flag was displayed from the business houses and private residences, and soon "music arose with its voluptuous swell."[82] For some time we could not comprehend the meaning of this commotion and feared that the Confederate army had won a great victory over our troops; or that England and France had recognized the Southern Confederacy. We soon learned, however, that the people of Richmond were celebrating the anniversary of the Battle of Bull Run. How little did our Confederate friends think that in less than three years their government would be a thing of the past, their president a fugitive, and their flag trailing in the dust.

Chapter 11

Discussing the Campaign

T HE VOLUNTEERS of the United States Army are altogether different men in point of intelligence from the soldiers of European countries. The rank and file of the armies of Europe are mainly made up from the lowest and most ignorant of the population. The soldier there is taught to obey orders, not to think. Even in the British Army it is a rare thing for a private to rise above the grade of a non-commissioned officer; and it is contrary to the army regulations for a general officer to mention in his report the name of any private who may have done something meritorious in battle.

During our Civil War, in fact, in all of our wars, the privates among the volunteers were in many cases better educated and more intelligent than the officers who commanded them. The last two generals who commanded the armies of the United States, as well as the present general, were privates in the War of the Rebellion.[83] Hence it has been well said that "The bayonet of the American private soldier thinks." During a campaign the private discusses the situation intelligently, and after a battle criticizes the causes of success or failure with as much intelligence as the general commanding.[84]

During the sixteen days that the prisoners lay on the battle ground of Gaines's Mill, as well as during their prison life in Richmond, they discussed the campaign daily. Comrade Lowry, who possessed the elements of a general, and would have risen to high command had his life spared, frequently discussed the errors and defects of McClellan's generalship. I do not know whether he ever read the battle of Austerlitz, but he always insisted that McClellan should have attacked Lee when the rebel army was divided, with a river between the two wings.[85] Had Grant, or Sherman, or Sheridan been in command of the Army of the Potomac in the Seven Days fight, the campaign would have had a different result.[86]

The difference in the character of the first and last commander of the Army of the Potomac was well illustrated at the beginning of the war. When President Lincoln issued his first general order, as commander-in-chief of the army, for a forward movement of all the armies, on the 22nd of February, McClellan did not move before the tenth of March; he had to delay obeying the president's order until the ground would dry. Grant, who construed the president's order to mean that he need not wait until the 22nd of February, was off within twenty-four hours after receiving the order, and by the 22nd of February had fought a great battle, and taken more prisoners than had ever been captured by any general on the American continent.[87]

Lee attempted the same maneuver on Grant at Spotsylvania which was so successful against McClellan on the Chickahominy. He massed on Grant's right and struck it a terrible blow. Grant and Meade were sitting on a log together, when an aide rode forward and informed Grant that Lee had massed on his right and was driving it by force of superior numbers. Grant handed the order to Meade, who became excited. Soon another and another aide rode forward with the same report. "My God, General," exclaimed Meade, "we will have to take the army out of here." Grant, as cool as "patience on a monument," took his hat off his head, the cigar out of his mouth, and said to himself: "Ah, Mr. Robert Lee, you are driving my right flank; I will see what I can do with your right flank," and wrote an order for a vigorous attack on Lee's right. Meade was ready to retreat; Grant had not begun to fight.[88]

Notwithstanding the failure of the campaign, McClellan was still the idol of the Army of the Potomac. In the tobacco warehouse the prisoners in ninety-nine cases in one hundred stood by him, and would allow no adverse criticism of his generalship. On one occasion, when Lowry and I were chatting together, a prisoner, an intelligent man, began discussing the campaign. He insisted that we had not been defeated; that the general had only changed his base, his position on the Chickahominy having become untenable. I said to him, "I wish I could think so; a general never fights a battle without an object in view; to do so is to sacrifice his men. It would have been much easier for the general to change his base before Stonewall Jackson's reinforcements arrived; then he could have saved his army stores, his artillery and his men. The facts are that McClellan was outgeneralled. We would have taken Richmond had the army been properly handled. We are better soldiers than the Rebels; were better clad; better fed; better drilled; more intelligent; it isn't our fault that Richmond was not taken." A hospital nurse, who had a light cane in his hand, walked over to me and raised it to strike me, declaring that he would allow no man to criticize General McClellan's generalship. Lowry asked me to let the matter drop, and turning to the hospital nurse said to him: "Comrade, you are wasting your valor in the wrong place; you should have used it in battle, where it was needed; but I very much doubt if you possess any of the article, or you would not raise your arm to strike a wounded man." The nurse, who had never fired a shot in battle, collapsed.[89]

Before the campaign opened I had lost faith in McClellan as an able general. He could do everything well but fight. His admirers called him "the Young Napoleon." There was never a more unfortunate comparison. When Napoleon took command of the Army of Italy it had been reduced to the lowest condition by suffering and poverty. Before starting out on the campaign Napoleon said to his friends: "In three weeks you will see me back in Paris or hear from me in Milan." In fifteen days he had won six battles, captured fifteen thousand prisoners, taken fifty-five pieces of artillery, and conquered the richest part of Piedmont.[90] When McClellan took command of the Army of the Potomac he said to his soldiers: "You have seen your last defeat; you have made your last retreat." He promised to make rapid marches and bring the war to a speedy close. He repeatedly promised to take Richmond, but was never ready to fight when the time came to redeem his promise. Instead of attacking Lee he waited until Lee attacked him and then fled for protection under cover of the gunboats on the James River.

In his history of his campaigns, entitled *McClellan's Own Story*, he gives as his main reason for not assuming the offensive on the south side of the Chickahominy, after Lee had detached [Jackson] to crush Fitz John Porter,[91] that he had on hand but a limited amount of rations, and as it would have taken some time to carry the strong works in his front his men would have been short of food.[92]

He gives the losses of the two armies in the series of battles known as the "Seven Days' Fight" as follows:

CONFEDERATES

Killed	2,822
Wounded	13,703
Missing	3,224
Total	19,749

ARMY OF THE POTOMAC

Killed	1,745
Wounded	8,062
Missing	6,042
Total	15,849 [93]

The above figures show that our army, in the series of battles, killed and wounded more Confederates than our combined losses of killed, wounded and missing; and McClellan reports that he won every battle except Gaines's Mill. This only increases the wonder that he turned his back upon the enemy after defeating him every time, except at Gaines's Mill. He insists that he was greatly out-numbered. We know now that he had more men than Lee.[94]

Nearly all of the Southern generals who fought against McClellan have said that they feared him more than any other general who commanded the Army of the Potomac, and that he struck them harder blows. This is probably correct; but it was due to the fact that the rank and file of the Army of the Potomac loved McClellan more than they loved any other commander, not even excepting Grant. Had McClellan possessed half of Grant's will and willingness to fight he would have finished up the war like a clap of thunder. Grant did not know how to retreat; McClellan did not know how to fight. There was always a lion in his path.

Chapter 12

Paroled

EVERY DAY AFTER the first two weeks of our confinement in the tobacco warehouse we expected to receive some positive information in regard to being paroled. Rumors were floating through the prison all hours of the day that we were to be released and sent North, and excitement was up to fever heat on the subject. Every time the director returned from a visit to the city he was besieged for news, and it was always encouraging.[95] The most extravagant expressions of joy were indulged in at the mention of these glad tidings. Wounds and sickness were forgotten and nothing was thought of but the prospect of returning to God's country. The change from our former despair to our present joy cannot well be described.

When we received positive information that the arrangements had been completed for our release a feeling of joyous exultation filled every breast in the prison. It was the happiest moment of our lives. When night came we could not sleep. Early the following morning the comrades standing at the windows saw a long file of prisoners from a tobacco warehouse above come marching down the street on the way to the railroad station. Next morning another long file passed, and in the evening we were notified that we would be released the following morning. I did not sleep a wink that night, and few eyes were closed in the building. All were up bright and early next morning, happy in the assurance that we were once more to breathe the sweet, pure air of heaven.[96]

Some of the prisoners belonging to the preceding gangs were obliged to return to their prison quarters until the following day, there being no room in the cars to convey them. Weak and crippled, I was determined not to get left and spend another night in that horrible black hole of Calcutta.[97] When the command was given, "Forward, march," I put forth all my strength to keep from falling behind, and was fortunate enough to reach the train before all the cars were filled; but I had to suffer afterwards for my temerity, as the over-exertion made me so feverish and sore that I could not walk without pain for two weeks.

Some good angel must have visited the dreaming ear of the railroad officials or Jeff Davis, for the train was made up of first-class, up-to-date passenger coaches. The train was no sooner loaded with its dirty, ragged, but supremely happy passengers than it started for City Point, where the prisoners were to be formally turned over to the Confederate States Officers appointed to receive them.[98] In about an hour we reached Petersburg, thirty miles south of Richmond, where a short stop was made.[99] An old darky, who was selling pies, came up to the window and I bought one of his pies, giving him in payment the last quarter of the Confederate money I had received for the regimental band belt in Richmond. The pie was horrible stuff and, after taking a bite, I threw it out of the window.

The train started up again and in twenty minutes reached City Point. As the wounded and emaciated soldiers of the Union beheld the Stars and Stripes floating from the masts of the steamboats in the river, loud shouts rent the air; and tears rolled down the cheeks of men unused to weeping. After the cheering subsided the paroled prisoners, with voices like Stentor, sang the doxology — and we certainly did "Praise God from Whom all Blessings Flow."[100]

After relieving their feelings in this manner the prisoners were transferred on board the steamboat *Commodore*, and were presented with new uniforms, consisting of cap, shoes, underwear, shirt, blouse, pants and socks.[101] We were assisted in undressing and given a good bath. I still wore the blouse I had on when I was wounded; it had two holes in it, one in front, the other in the rear, where the ball entered and passed through my left side. I did not think of it at the time or I would have asked the officer in command to allow me to retain it as a war relic. All the clothing of the prisoners was wrapped up in bundles and flung into the river.

The same evening we were carried to Harrison's Landing, and on the way passed the gunboat flotilla. The little *Monitor*, called the "Yankee Cheesebox," from the shape of its turret, was an object of special wonder and admiration.[102] When the *Commodore* reached Harrison's Landing, where the Army of the Potomac was camped, it hove to and tied up for the night.[103]

Among the nurses on the boat there was a young and beautiful Quaker girl, whose voice was sweet, gentle and low. She always said "thee" and "thou" in speaking. She was well educated and belonged to one of the best families in Philadelphia. The prisoners idolized her. Some of the more chivalrous declared that it was worth all the suffering and privation they had endured in the rebel prison to look upon her pretty face, and hear her sweet, low and gentle voice.[104]

Not having slept a wink the preceding night, I had promised myself a good night's sleep tonight, and stretched myself on my cot, which was soft and clean — the sheets being white as the driven snow; but hour after hour passed away and I could not sleep. Comfortable as was my bed I was not comfortable. The luxury of a good bed was too great to be enjoyed. At midnight I slipped out of bed, stretched my body full length on the bare floor of the boat, and in a few minutes was sound asleep, and did not waken until called for breakfast.

Chapter 13

A Visit from the General

AFTER BREAKFAST the following morning all the wounded and sick were ordered to bed in their respective cots, with the statement that General McClellan was coming on board to see his boys. A visit from the general of the army to a lot of returned prisoners of war was an event not of common occurrence, and in no other country would it be regarded as proper. But all men are equal in the eye of God and by the Constitution of the United States.

The General came aboard about nine in the forenoon, and remained all day conversing with the prisoners. He shook hands with every one, inquired about their wounds or sickness, the kind of treatment they received in the Rebel prisons, and gave a minute or two of his time to each. As he approached my cot one of the boys said to him: "General, we got into Richmond ahead of you." The General colored to the eyes; the soldier meant it as a pleasantry, but the stroke was too practical to be enjoyed. He took me by the hand as he had done others and inquired where I was wounded, lifted the cover from the wound, and asked if I had suffered much. I answered that "I had suffered terribly, but had tried to bear up as became a soldier." He inquired what regiment I belonged to; I answered, "The Tenth Pennsylvania Reserves," and asked him how the Reserves behaved in the series of battles. "Splendidly," he replied. I asked him "What was your loss in men in the campaign?" "About thirteen thousand." Said I, "General, has the result of the campaign discouraged you?" He raised his arm above his head, swung it in a circle for emphasis, and exclaimed with great earnestness of feeling: "We will put this Rebellion down as sure as the sun shines in Heaven."

It was late in the evening when General McClellan left the boat. His visit pleased the boys greatly; his robust figure, his keen eye and broad forehead, his soldierly bearing, kind manner, and his confidence that the Rebellion would be put down, endeared him more than ever to the boys, who had fought with rare heroism and suffered untold privation in Rebel prisons that the nation might live. Wounded and sick would, at his command, have left their cots to follow him to death or victory.

General McClellan appreciated the love and confidence the prisoners manifested on the occasion of his visits to them. In a private letter to his wife, written at nine o'clock the same evening of his visit, he says: "From nine o'clock this morning until six thirty this evening I have been among the sick and wounded. More than a thousand came from Richmond last night and were in the steamer. I saw every one of the poor fellows, talked to them all, heard their sorrows, tried to cheer them up, and feel that I have done my duty toward them. If you could have seen the poor, brave fellows, some at the point of death, brightening up when they saw me, and caught me by the hand, it would have repaid you for much of our common grief and anxiety. It has been the most harrowing day I have passed, yet a proud one for me; and I trust many a poor fellow will sleep more soundly and feel more happy tonight for my visit to them. It makes them feel that they are not forgotten or neglected when their general comes to see them and console them. My men love me very much."[105]

The change of fortune which had befallen the prisoners in the past twenty-four hours was more like some Oriental tale than a reality.[106] Yesterday imprisoned in a foul and filthy tobacco warehouse, breathing an atmosphere so charged with nephritic vapor that one could not draw a full inspiration; our bodies covered with loathsome vermin; half starved; without proper medical attendance to dress the wounded or minister to the sick. Today breathing the sweet, fresh air; divested of our ragged, dirty and populous clothes; our bodies washed clean, dressed in new uniforms, sailing down a majestic river on a floating palace; sitting down to food not surpassed in the president's dining room, served to us by beautiful and cultured ladies, and honored by a visit from the general of the army, who was proud to take every returned common soldier by the hand.[107]

Cut off from all communication in our gloomy prison house in Richmond, none of us knew anything about the great changes which had recently been made among the army commanders — that General McClellan had been superseded as commander-in-chief of the army by General Halleck; that the department of Virginia had been created and placed in command of General Pope, leaving General McClellan in command of only such troops as were at Harrison's Landing. These changes in commanders were, as events demonstrated, all for the worse. Halleck was greatly inferior to McClellan as commander-in-chief, and Pope was rash and a braggart. The second Bull Run was a greater disaster than the first.[108]

McClellan had been ordered to withdraw his command to Acquia creek, at the time he called on the paroled prisoners, who were under the impression that he was getting ready for another campaign against Richmond. He had protested against the order to withdraw, and had asked for another chance to move against Richmond; but no attention had been paid to his protestations or entreaties. He had lost the confidence of the administration, but the soldiers under his command believed in him and loved him as much as ever. As usual, he was not ready to move to Acquia creek when ordered, and when he did move it was too late to render Pope any assistance.[109]

Chapter 14

Fortress Monroe

S HORTLY AFTER General McClellan left us the *Commodore* backed out into the middle of the river and headed for Fortress Monroe. All the sick and wounded on the boat did sleep sounder that night from the visit of General McClellan. The clean, soft bed on which I could not sleep the previous night was not an obstacle now. Like Goldsmith's sailor, "I loved to lie soft," and slept like a top.[110] The steamer reached the Fortress early in the afternoon.

As the paroled prisoners stepped off the boat reporters representing the large daily newspapers took the name, regiment and residence of each. In the hurry of transcribing many inaccuracies necessarily crept into the papers. My name was printed "A. Ray, 16th Regiment, Pa. Reserves, Residence Frostburg, Missouri." A younger brother translated this to mean "A. Roy, 10th Pa. Reserves, Frostburg, Md." But mother found no comfort in the translation. She knew I was dead, because shortly after I was wounded a small piece of plaster fell from the ceiling on her head. This, she insisted, was a warning to her that I had died that moment. She was of Highland descent and was quite superstitious.

The severely wounded were assigned to quarters in the fort, which had been converted into a hospital. The convalescents were forwarded to Camp Parole, near Annapolis, Maryland, or to the General Hospital in the Naval Academy, according to their condition.

I was left in the hospital at Fortress Monroe, and was still weak and feverish from the effects of the walk from the prison to the depot in Richmond. Comrade Lowry also remained at the fortress for a week or two.[111]

From the day of the battle of Gaines's Mill to the present time I had not been able to get a letter sent through the lines. I had learned that some of the comrades of the company had written mother that I had been mortally wounded and left in the hands of the enemy, and I often thought of the sorrow which these letters would cause her. I procured pen and paper and wrote a long letter to her, informing her of my return to God's country, after being made prisoner at the battle of Gaines's Mill, that I had been badly wounded in the battle and was reported in the regiment to have died from the effects of my wound; but, while severely wounded, I had pulled through all right and hoped soon to be able to get a furlough and get home to see her. In the course of a week I received her reply to the letter, in which she told me that after receiving my comrades' letters, stating that I had been mortally wounded, she had mourned me as dead. She had been wearing mourning and was as much surprised at the receipt of my letter as if I had risen out of the grave before her eyes. I had inherited a very rugged constitution from my ancestors and, besides, had never lost hope of recovering, which the doctors say is a very strong point in one's favor, when death would fain invade this earthly tabernacle.

It took about two weeks to bring me back to the same degree of strength that I possessed when I made the long walk from the prison to the railroad station in Richmond. I took daily strolls along the bay. The balmy air was so bracing that I soon began to hope that in the course of nine or ten weeks I would be fully recovered from my wound; in this hope I was encouraged by the surgeon of the hospital, who was not aware that there were dead bones in the wound. The surgeon never probed the wound all the time that I was at the Fortress.

Comrade Lowry, to whom I had become as strongly attached as if he had been my twin brother, was sent to Camp Parole, near Annapolis, Maryland, as a convalescent. He wrote me a characteristic letter from Camp Parole concerning the recent changes in army commanders and predicted the speedy collapse of General Pope, who had dated his first general order from "Headquarters in the Saddle." General Lee, who was a grave and dignified man, perpetrated the only joke of his life when he read this order, saying that it was the first time that a general had his headquarters where his hindquarters ought to be.[112]

I greatly enjoyed living at Fortress Monroe. The clean, soft bed, the substantial, well-prepared rations, the pure, clear, cold water, compared with the miserable half ration, hot and dirty drinking water, the filthy tobacco stained floor teeming with vermin, the polluted atmosphere, reeking with stench, was as pronounced as the upper and lower regions described in the Book of God.[113]

Every care and attention were given the thin and emaciated soldiers, and all improved rapidly. Although I was gradually gaining in strength, the wound continued to discharge the same amount of matter. I could not understand the reason, and frequently consulted the doctor about it, who invariably told me to have patience and I would soon be well.

I remained in Fortress Monroe for three or four weeks, then becoming impatient that the wound did not heal faster than it did, suggested to the surgeon in charge to transfer me to Camp Parole, which he readily agreed to do. It was much nearer to my mother's home, and I thought that the chance of getting a furlough to visit her, or at least to get a transfer to the General Hospital, at Clarysville, Maryland, two miles from her home, might be brought about at Annapolis in case the wound did not heal as soon as I hoped it would.

I duly received the transfer and was conveyed to Annapolis, the quaint old capital of Maryland, thence to Camp Parole.[114] I immediately hunted up my friend Lowry, and spent the night with him in his tent. The paroled prisoners were living in tents like troops in the field. Those who were too weak from sickness or wounds were sent to the General Hospital in the navy yard. There were several thousand paroled troops in camp, some few of them being of the company to which I belonged, who had been captured in the later battles of the Peninsula.

Fearing that the hard fare incident to life in the tented field would be more than I could stand, Comrade Lowry advised me not to think of remaining at Camp Parole; but to report to the examining surgeon and get into the General Hospital in the Naval Academy. Accordingly, the next morning I washed my wound carefully and clean, put a clean bandage about my body and reported to the surgeon for examination. He was a Scotchman, dressed in the Highland trousers, worn by the Seventy-ninth New York Highlanders; and it did not take long to discover that he possessed his full share of Highland pride. After examining my wound, he told me to go to Camp Parole. "Doctor," said I, "Do you not think that I should be sent to the Navy Yard Hospital?" "O, no," he replied, "that wound is almost well; report at Camp Parole."

Returning to the camp, I hunted up the members of my company, and passed the balance of the day with them. They were agreeably surprised to see me, as they thought I was dead. The following morning I did not dress my wound, and the bandage was covered with pus. In this condition I again reported to the surgeon, who, after unwrapping the bandage, which was reeking with matter, asked, "What are you doing here? You should be in the Navy Yard." "Doctor," said I, "you examined my wound yesterday and sent me to Camp Parole." "I din no such thing," he answered testily, and immediately wrote out an order for my admittance to the General Hospital, in the Navy Yard.[115]

The Seventy-ninth New York Highlanders, to which the surgeon belonged, was largely composed of men of Scottish birth or descent. The first colonel of the regiment was John Cameron, a brother of the Secretary of War. The regiment came to Washington, dressed in full Highland costume; it soon discarded the kilt, and wore plaid pants and coat. Colonel Cameron was killed at the first battle of Bull Run, fighting gallantly at the head of his regiment, "as high and wild the Cameron's pibroch rose, the war-note of Lochiel."[116]

The Seventy-ninth Highlanders were later sent to South Carolina, and occupied a fort, two or three hundred yards in front of which there ran a ravine. Soon afterward a Union scout reported to the colonel that a Rebel brigade would attack the fort during the night. The regiment drove stakes in front of the fort, stretched a series of lines of wire from one stake to another and awaited the foe. The moon was shining bright as the Confederates came out of the ravine and formed in close column of division. They gave the Rebel yell and charged on the double quick, but never reached the fort, falling in promiscuous confusion over the wires. The Union regiment opened a murderous fire, the Rebels sprang to their feet, and made a precipitate retreat. It was the tactics of Bruce at the battle of Bannockburn repeated.[117]

Chapter 15

The Naval Academy

ANNAPOLIS IS AN old seaport town, but was too near Baltimore to secure foreign trade, and is still a mere village. Some of the houses were built of brick, imported from England 250 years ago. It is the capital of Maryland; and the seat of the United States Naval Academy, which was built in 1845, and has trained some of the greatest naval commanders of any age or nation.[118] During the War of the Rebellion it was converted into the more humane business of saving lives. I was assigned to a ward on the second story of one of the buildings. As soon as the nurse had washed my wound the surgeon inserted his probe in the rear orifice, exercising great care and caution in moving it forward. After pushing the probe in for about three inches, he said "I am now through the bone; the ball has passed through the center of it, and I find some necrosis bone."[119] I knew that the bone had been struck, but was not aware that the ball had passed through it.

After he had withdrawn the probe he wrote two words on a card in Latin meaning gunshot wound, and placed it at the head of my bed.[120] "What position were you in when you were shot?" he asked. "Charging bayonets," I answered.

"Well," said he, "You were in the act of stepping with your left foot, and the weight of your body was resting on your right leg, and that position saved your life; had you been on the other foot your bowels would have been cut."[121]

"Why, doctor," said I, "The rebel surgeon who dressed the wound, after I was made prisoner, told me that I could not live three days, and our own surgeon, who dressed it the evening of the battle reported the wound fatal. How long will it be before I am fit for duty?"

"I cannot tell positively," he answered. "The dead bone will have to decompose before the wound will stop discharging, and it may be several months before this will occur."

"Can an operation not be performed and the dead bone removed?" I inquired. "No sir," he replied, "an operation would kill you, the wound is so near a vital spot."

All this was a revelation, and greatly dampened my ardor of getting well soon.

When I entered the Navy Yard Hospital I had not one cent of money; but I needed none, for everything necessary for the pleasure and comfort of the sick and wounded was provided by the government, even the soldier's letters were sent free. A soldier once sent the following rhyme on his envelope:

> Soldier's letter — push it ahead
> Hard tack and no good bread,
> Five months' pay due and ne'er a red.

Still one likes to have a little change in his pockets, even if he does not find it necessary to spend it, so I wrote to a friend and asked him to send me ten dollars until I should be paid by Uncle Sam. There was five months' pay due me, but a descriptive list was necessary from the captain of the company before I could draw it. The captain had been shot through the body and made prisoner in one of the later battles of the Seven Days' Fight and I knew not where to write him.[122]

My friend promptly answered my letter enclosing ten dollars, but it was some little time before I received it. One day I was strolling leisurely through the navy yard when three soldiers passed me and separated. In doing so one of them said, "Good bye, Roy."

"Well," said I, "that is my name."

One of the soldiers turned to me and inquired if my first name was Andrew, and on being answered in the affirmative, he informed me that there was a letter in the post office for me, containing ten dollars.

"My name," said he, "is Augustus Roy, and thinking that the letter was for me I opened it, but finding it was for another Roy I sealed it again, and you will find everything all right by inquiring at the post office."

Augustus Roy, who had come to the hospital before me, belonged to

Company F, Tenth Massachusetts Volunteers, and I belonged to Company F, Tenth Pennsylvania Volunteers, so that there was similarity in both names and companies. I called at the Post Office and got the letter and the ten dollars. Later I got a letter addressed to A. Roy, with neither company nor regiment on the address, and opened it. It was written in French, a language which I did not understand, so I took it to Augustus Roy, who read it with great facility. He then told me that he was the son of a Frenchman and had learned to read and write the language in boyhood, and that the letter was from his father.[123]

A few days after my arrival I called on the general surgeon of the hospital, and requested to be transferred to the General Hospital, at Clarysville, Maryland, which was situated within two miles of my mother's home. He informed me that he had not the authority to grant the transfer; and that I would have to write to the Department in Washington. I did so, but received no reply. I then wrote to some influential friends in Frostburg, Maryland, who interested themselves to secure the transfer, but it took several months before all the red tape conditions were complied with and the transfer brought about.[124]

In the meantime I was getting acquainted with the sick and wounded comrades in the ward. They were nearly all from the Army of the Potomac, the volunteers which comprised McClellan's army having been largely drawn from Pennsylvania and the states further East. Quite a number were from the New England states, and were shrewd and intelligent fellows. There was a wiry little Yankee from the state of Connecticut, in the ward, who was a man after my own heart. He was intensely patriotic and had been a reader of books. His home was in Litchfield, a town named in honor of the celebrated Dr. Johnson.[125] The inhabitants of Litchfield were proud of the name and were people of unusual intelligence. The little Yankee, whose name I have forgotten, and I became great friends. We had read the same books and were mainly in accord as to the great poets which Great Britain and the United States had produced.

In discussing the war and its results, my friend insisted that the South was more terribly in earnest than we were, and that their enthusiasm was in a great measure making up for their lack of resources. We needed a battle cry that would inspire our troops, he insisted. "The Preservation of the Union" did not appeal to men's patriotism like the word "Subjugation" to the Southerner. He could not think of a suitable war cry, but he knew that one was needed. We passed hours together nearly every day, and he often whiled away the heavy hours of hospital life telling amusing incidents touching the characters of his native town.

There were provided for the inmates of the various wards, books and newspapers, dominoes, checkers, and other innocent games for recreation and amusement. I was fond of playing checkers; there were four or five players in the ward of equal skill; our contests, which were frequent, were watched with keen interest by our associates in the ward. One of these was a German, who did not understand the game, but took great interest in the result, looking on patiently during its progress — and he always knew who came out victor, because, said he, "The loser always throws down his checkers first."

One of the inmates of our ward, who was a convalescent, possessed a fine taste for the beautiful in art and nature. He loved to saunter in the town and country by himself to indulge his taste. One day he was admiring a fine house, when the head of it came out and invited him in to dinner. The young soldier, who was modest and bashful, declined. The gentleman, however, would take no excuse, and the young soldier finally followed him into the imposing mansion. He was introduced to the company present, among whom were several elegant ladies. He was in mortal dread lest his table manners would provoke remark. When he left after dinner, the gentleman followed him to the door, shook hands with him, cordially invited him to come back again, and bring some of his comrades with him. On his return to the navy yard he related the circumstance to the comrades in the ward, and was struck dumb when he was told that he had dined with the governor of Maryland.[126]

Meanwhile my wound continued to run as freely as ever; the surgeon probed it every few days, exercising the utmost care in inserting the probe in the front orifice. Small pieces of bone began to work out at the rear opening, which encouraged the surgeon to think that nature, which he said was the best surgeon, would soon throw off the dead bone, and he informed me that I could not hope to recover until all the bone had worked out.

Notwithstanding my emaciated condition, I had gained considerable strength since being admitted to the navy yard, and although Camp Parole was a mile or more from the hospital, I was able, by walking slowly and taking several rests on the way, to visit the camp, and to pass a few hours with the comrades of my company. There was one man among them who had fallen out of the ranks on the firing line at Gaines Mill and felt the reproaches of his comrades keenly. In all the subsequent battles in which the regiment participated he nobly redeemed himself. The first time I met him at the camp he exclaimed: "Roy, I showed the white feather at Gaines Mill, but I have fought bravely in every battle since." Poor fellow, he was killed in the last battle that the regiment took part in, it being the eighteenth in which he had fought.[127]

My friends in Frostburg, Maryland, had been in communication for several months with the medical authorities touching my transfer to the Clarysville Hospital, and after many letters written and received succeeded in bringing it about. Before the transfer reached me the paroled prisoners were exchanged, and early in December all able for duty were notified to report to their respective regiments. I made a trip out to Camp Parole to pass a day with them before they left. Comrade Lowry, who had often visited me in the navy yard, had long chafed at the dull, aimless life at the camp. He received a new lease on life when the news came that he was to be sent to the front; indeed, all the comrades were inspired with the same feeling.

When Lowry reached the regiment at Falmouth it was in line of battle, awaiting the order to cross the Rappahannock on the pontoon bridges for Fredericksburg. The captain of his company ordered him to remain in camp until the regiment crossed the river, as he had not time to get him a musket and accouterments. Lowry found a sick soldier in camp, borrowed his musket and belts, and fell into line just as the company was about to step on the pontoons. He was killed in battle, shot through the heart, and thus died all unknown to fame, a man competent to command an army corps, and who, had his life been spared, would have risen to high command.[128]

Chapter 16

Clarysville

TOWARD THE LAST of December I received transfer and transportation papers to the General Hospital at Clarysville, Maryland, and bidding good-bye to all my friends, started on my journey.[129] The weather was bitter cold, and I had but little money, only a few dollars of the ten which I had borrowed when I entered the navy yard, for I had yet received no pay from Uncle Sam. I took passage via the Pennsylvania Central as the Baltimore & Ohio road had recently been torn up by Rebel raids. I left the railroad at Hopewell and went the rest of the way by stage, stopping all night at Bedford, in Pennsylvania. The landlord of the hotel had an autograph letter of President Buchanan in the office show-case.

The bed to which I was assigned had but one thin covering; the night was cold and my body was well drained of blood from long suffering. I could not sleep, but lay shivering with cold the whole night and thought morning would never come. I reached Cumberland, Maryland, ten miles distant, the following afternoon, and put up at the home of a Union widow, who I had been informed was kind to soldiers. After breakfast the next morning, on inquiring for my bill, mine hostess replied, "Nothing." I insisted on paying her, but she would not take the money, saying that she had two sons in the Union army and that she never charged a soldier for a meal or a night's lodging.

As the train on the branch road to Clarysville did not leave until the afternoon I walked over to see some acquaintances in the Second Maryland regiment of the Potomac Home Brigade, which was stationed in the town. Lieutenant Andrew Spiers, an old and valued friend, was very kind; he tendered me all the money I needed, and felt hurt because

I did not accept his offer to loan me a hundred dollars which he urged upon me, without note or interest, and to be paid back at such time as I wished to return the money.[130]

Lieutenant Spiers and I had worked in the same mine together before the war. He was the most intelligent and scholarly miner I ever knew. He was a great reader of books. We used to meet after our day's work in the mine and read aloud to each other, fifteen minutes alternately. In this manner we read Allison's History of Europe, Bancroft's history of the United States and a number of Shakespeare's plays, Burns's Poetry, *Childe Harold's Pilgrimage, Paradise Lost,* Longfellow and Bryant.[132]

I took the cars in the afternoon on the branch road to Clarysville and on my arrival immediately reported to Surgeon J. B. Lewis in charge of the General Hospital, who treated me with great kindness and consideration, permitting me to go home and report to Doctor Townsend once a week. I was driven home the same evening and met my mother, who could hardly realize that I could be alive. The cup of joy was full to running over with both of us.[132]

Dr. Townsend, the assistant surgeon at the Clarysville hospital, was a practicing physician at Eckhart Mines and Vale Summit when the war broke out, and had been our family physician.[133] He still kept up his practice in both of the above named villages, and every time he visited Vale Summit called to dress my wound. He provided mother with a syringe, and directed her to use it in the wound twice a day, with milk-warm water, saturated with castile soap; and to invariably insert the point of the syringe in the rear orifice.[134] The water, when shot into the wound, would fly out at the front in a stream and land several feet beyond the point of exit. The neighbors, when informed of the fact, hesitated to believe, and came in numbers to witness the strange sight.

Dr. Townsend, in probing the wound, used the utmost care and caution in inserting his instrument. He, like the surgeon at the Naval Academy Hospital, thought that the wound was too near a vital point to be examined except with the utmost care, and said it was little less than a miracle that the bowels were not cut when I was shot.

The syringing did not help me much, and as the winter passed into spring I became impatient and insisted on an operation to remove the dead bone. He would not for a moment entertain the idea, declaring that it would kill me; that the only way to get well was to allow nature to work out her remedy in her own way; that nature is the best surgeon; and I would have to bide her time. To the question, "How long will nature take to rid the wound of the dead bone?" he replied, "It will be several months."

A valued friend, Alexander Sloan, a mine boss at Vale Summit, had presented me shortly after I came home with a fine, stout cane, which was my constant companion in my walks around the village.

A few months after my wound healed up Comrade Joseph Stewart,[135] who had been wounded in the same battle with me and borne off the battlefield in the same ambulance, selected me as "bestman," and his sister as "bestmaid," for his wedding.[136] The wedding party consisted of twenty-five or thirty lads and lassies, and all went to Cumberland, the county seat, where the happy couple were made one flesh.

Immediately after the performance of the marriage ceremony the party adjourned to the Queen City Hotel for dinner. Two of the girls were without escorts, and by an oversight were not invited to dinner. As soon as my attention was called to the matter, I immediately rose from the table to look for the girls and found them on Baltimore street standing by themselves. I apologized for the oversight, taking all the blame, and courteously invited them to dinner; one of them snappishly thanked me and said "they had money enough to purchase their own dinner," and stubbornly declined my invitation, and I had to return to the Hotel without them.

Before the passenger coach left Cumberland for the mines I bought a number of apples and oranges, and gave each girl of the party an orange and an apple, and the two girls without escorts two apiece, and again apologized for the oversight. They accepted the fruit and the apology, and we all whirled up the sinuous mountain side as merry as a marriage bell, to Vale Summit.

After supper the wedding party adjourned to the village hall where arrangements had been made to trip the light fantastic toe. I sought out the high-spirited girl and sat down beside her. She asked me to tell her the story of my prison life. Like Othello I ran it through "even to the present moment that she bade me tell it":[137] How I had been wounded and "taken prisoner by the insolent foe," and had been left for dead on the battle-field; how my comrades had written mother, informing her that I had been mortally wounded and left on the battle-field; how I had been left with thousands of other prisoners for sixteen days on the battle-field without medical attention, my wound filled with maggots; with no clothing but my blouse; then taken to Richmond and confined to a tobacco warehouse with over eight hundred comrades, all so closely huddled together that men died every day by the score; our bodies being covered with pestiferous vermin; and half starved.

My story being finished, she gave me for my pains a world of thanks, like Desdemona in the play.

> Upon this hint I spoke
> She loved me for the dangers I had passed
> And I loved her that she did pity me.

We were married on the 21st of July, 1864, just two years from the date of my enlistment.[138]

Lieutenant Spiers would frequently come up from Cumberland to pass the day with me, and read Shakespeare and Burns and I was not all unhappy, although I did at times betray marked impatience at the slow surgical progress of old mother nature.[139]

After thirteen months of weary waiting, I received a payment from Uncle Sam.[140] The soldiers were being paid thirteen dollars a month, and I received 156 dollars. At this time the greenbacks had reached the lowest point in depreciation, a dollar in greenbacks being worth thirty-three cents in gold, so that as a matter of fact I received but fifty-two dollars instead of 156. The capitalists who loaned the government money to carry on the war were paid principal and interest in gold or its equivalent; in other words, they were paid a hundred cents on the dollar, while the poor soldier was paid but thirty-three cents on the dollar. This always looked to me to be grossly unfair on the part of the government. The man who bared his breast that the government might live was entitled to the same pay as the man who loaned the government money — the same pay and no more. The government, however, has made amends for its treatment of her gallant soldiers in the bounties and liberal pensions which she has given them since the close of the war.

Maryland was a slave state before the war, and many of the citizens were Rebels at heart; Vale Summit had its quota of these pestiferous copperheads. One day a member of the Second Maryland Potomac

Janet Watson

Roy met this "high-spirited girl" in 1863 at the wedding of his comrade Joseph Stewart, who had also been wounded at Gaines's Mill. She stood for this portrait when she was eighteen, about the time of her engagement to Roy, who was eleven or twelve years her senior. They were married July 21, 1864.

Home Brigade came into mother's house with a musket in his hand, and anger on his face, and asked me to let him have a cap; "I am after a copperhead who is hurrahing for Jeff Davis. When my wife saw me loading my musket she hid the caps."[141] I took hold of his gun to see that the powder was up in the tube, put on a cap and handed it back. There were a dozen or more copperheads standing together up the street. The soldier went toward them; one of the crowd took to his heels and sought safety in an adjoining store, and locked the door. The soldier burst the door open with the butt of his musket; but it was too late; the bird had flown, having found egress through a back window, and taken to the woods. The circumstances were, however, reported to the provost marshal of Cumberland who sent a file of soldiers to arrest the copperhead.[142] He was thrown into the military prison of the department and given ample time to reflect on the tyranny of the Lincoln government.

In the early part of the summer of 1863, finding that I was not improving any I consulted Dr. Lewis, the surgeon in charge of the Clarysville Hospital, in regard to an operation to remove the dead bone from my wound, stating that if there was one chance in a hundred of surviving the operation I was willing to take that chance. He answered that there was not one chance in a hundred; that an operation would kill me beyond a doubt; and advised me to go back home, and have patience; that nature in its own good time would throw off the necrosis bone, and I would get well.

"How long will it be doctor before nature will do this work?" I inquired.

"It will not be many months longer," he answered in about the same words as Dr. Townsend, the assistant surgeon whom I had previously consulted.

Chapter 17

Surgical Operations

ONE OF THE DOCTORS in Frostburg, named James Porter, who, when I was a boy, was our family physician, stopped in to see me nearly every time professional business called him to the village of Vale Summit.[143] He stood high in the profession; was a man of a very high sense of honor, and had a heart of the finest water. He was the best representative of the "Doctor of the Old School" of Ian McLaren's story of "Beside the Bonnie Briar Bush," that I ever knew.[144] He loved his profession and answered every call, without considering the chances of being paid. I asked his opinion of the chances of recovery, in case an operation was performed on my wound. "I do not know," he frankly replied, "and there is not a surgeon around these mountains who does, but none of them will confess the fact; I see you are getting very impatient, and if you wish I will give you a letter to Dr. Smith of Baltimore; he is the best surgeon in the United States. If an operation can be performed with safety he will do it; if it cannot, he will tell you, and put your mind at ease."[145]

Armed with Doctor Porter's letter I went to Cumberland to consult Colonel Porter of the Second Maryland with whom I was well acquainted, in regard to transportation to Baltimore. He was a nephew of Dr. James Porter, and was himself a physician and surgeon by profession.[146] He and the surgeon of the regiment examined the wound carefully; they had the skeleton of a man in the surgeon's closet, hung together with wires, which they brought out and studied.[147] Finally the surgeon said to me: "You may as well return home; neither Dr. Smith of Baltimore, or any other surgeon living can operate on that wound without producing fatal results." Colonel Porter rather thought otherwise, and intimated that if he were in practice he would not fear to undertake it, and cut the wound on the outer rear side.

"Well," I replied, "I am going to Baltimore if transportation is furnished." Colonel Porter promised to see General Kelly, who was expected to be in the city in the evening; but did not come, and I stayed over night with Lieutenant Spiers.[148] In the morning Colonel Porter asked me if I felt strong enough to take a prisoner to the Rifrafs in Baltimore, who had been sentenced to six months imprisonment there for desertion.[149] All I would have do was to carry a loaded musket, and see that the prisoner, who would be handcuffed, did not get away from me; and the colonel promised to send Lieutenant Spiers along with me. I, of course, gladly accepted the proposition.

After handing the prisoner over to the military authorities in Baltimore, Lieutenant Spiers accompanied me to Dr. Smith's office. There were a number of patients in the office, and I had to wait my turn. I presented Dr. Porter's letter to the great surgeon and awaited in breathless suspense, until he finished reading it, then said: "Doctor, shall I show you the wound?"

"Certainly," he replied.

All the surgeons, civil and military, who had before probed the wound, inserted the instrument with caution, particularly when probing in front, because they said it was so near a vital point. Dr. Smith rammed his probe in front with great boldness and without the least regard for my feelings; then withdrawing it thrust it in the rear opening. "There is some necrosis bone in there; I will take it out and you will get well," he said. He sent for some students, spoke to them touching the nature of the wound, and rammed his forceps in the front orifice. He pulled out a piece of bone an inch in length and half an inch broad, looked at it a moment or two, thrust his forceps in again, and brought out a second piece as large as the first. The process was very painful. He looked in my face for a moment and in went the forceps again. After he had extracted seven pieces of bone, I said, "Doctor, for God's sake allow me a few moments to rest, and a drink of water, for I feel like fainting." He extracted fourteen pieces altogether, and although he probed the wound carefully could find no more.[150] He then said to me: "What made you come to me? Why did not your own surgeons extract these bones? Don't you know that I am a rebel?"

"O, doctor," I said, "you are no Rebel?"

"Yes, I am," he replied.

He charged me ten dollars for the operation. One of the students told me that the doctor had recently operated on the governor of Maryland, for stone in the bladder, and that it took more time to perform the operation on me than on the governor; but he charged him six hundred dollars. Wrapping up the pieces of bone, Lieutenant Spiers drove me to the depot, and I returned home.[151]

During my absence, Dr. Townsend, the assistant surgeon of the Clarysville Hospital, got word that I had gone to Baltimore to submit to an operation. He called on mother to verify the statement, and told her that I would be brought home a corpse. As a matter of duty I ought to have asked leave from the surgeon at Clarysville to make the visit to Baltimore, but I knew he would not consent; and I had to steal away or not go at all. I returned a very lively corpse, and was never called to account for what I had done. Dr. Townsend's statement had frightened mother, who was mourning a second time for me as dead.

Dr. Smith had told me, in answer to my inquiry, that the wound would heal up in five or six weeks; but although the flow of pus soon became greatly diminished it did not gradually lessen and cease altogether. At the end of ten weeks the wound was discharging as freely as it did the first week or two after the operation, and I made another trip to Baltimore to consult the professor.[152] He had forgotten me in the multitude of patients which he had treated, but soon recalled the case. He probed the wound, inserted his forceps and brought out a small piece of decayed bone, which he looked at quizzically;[153] tried the forceps again, but could find nothing more. He said: "that wound *must* heal up," and advised me to return home and have patience.

Notwithstanding the positive assurance of the learned surgeon the wound refused to heal. Week after week passed away, until the summer gave place to fall and the flow of matter had not diminished. But the heart of youth is not easily discouraged, and I resolved to try another surgeon.

Chapter 18

Another Surgical Operation

WITHOUT ADVISING with any of my friends, I resolved to go to Pittsburgh, Pennsylvania, and consult some surgeon there. I went by way of the Baltimore & Ohio railroad to Wheeling, W. Va. The train stopped at Wellsville for dinner; the proprietor of the Hotel was George Bean, who was a member of the same company, and was wounded in the same battle with me.[154] He had been shot in the knee, and when the wound healed it left him with a stiff leg; and being no longer fit for duty, he was discharged. He declined to charge me for dinner, stating that it was compensation enough to meet an old comrade in arms, and wished me good success in the proposed operation which I was about to undergo.

When the train started after dinner, I engaged in conversation with the passenger who occupied the same seat with me. He proved to be a resident of Pittsburgh; and in answer to my inquiry in regard to the name of a first-class surgeon, he recommended Dr. Walters; and informed me that the doctor kept a private hospital, in which I could stay until I recovered sufficiently from the operation to return home.

Dr. Walters carefully and cautiously probed the wound, and said he could find no necrosis bone, but there was some foreign substance in it, probably a piece of my blouse, and that he would have to make an incision to get it out. I told him nothing of the former operations of Professor Smith of Baltimore, and cared little what Dr. Walters proposed to do, so that he got out the foreign substance which was irritating the wound and preventing it from healing up.[155]

He made an incision at each orifice; then thrust his two middle fingers in the wound until they met. The process was terribly painful. I was lying on a dissecting table, and caught both sides of it with my hands, closed my teeth tightly together and resolved that no exclamation of pain should escape from my lips. After removing his hands he inserted his forceps and pulled out, not a piece of my blouse, but a good sized piece of dead bone. A second insertion of the forceps was rewarded with another piece. He could find no more with his forceps so he inserted his fingers again, but found nothing. I was suffering so much that I feared that I would faint. He gave me a spoonful of some liquid, which soon relieved me of the terrible pain.[156]

I have always thought that Doctor Smith, of Baltimore, unwittingly buried those bones that Dr. Walters removed. He had hold of a piece of bone with his forceps, the fifth or sixth insertion, which slipped from them as he was pulling it out and it was buried in the left side in the flesh, I think. He tore out the bones, one after another, with all the force he could command, which was, after all, the most merciful way to extract them. At the time I called his attention to the fact that one of the bones was buried, but he would not listen to me. I believe that it was a piece of this same bone, which had rotted off, which he removed when I went back to him the second time. It had rotted in two when Dr. Walters extracted it. He could not find it with his probe, it was too far in the flesh to attract his attention. Indeed, Dr. Smith was puzzled when he probed the wound on my second visit. Men who become eminent in any profession, make as serious mistakes as those of lesser attainments. When President Garfield was shot the surgeons could not locate the ball, and would not listen to the family physician who had diagnosed the case right. It is a question whether or not the celebrated surgeons in their futile efforts to locate the ball did not kill the brave, long-suffering president.[157]

After the operation, I stayed several days in the hospital being too weak to make the journey home. On the third or fourth day a miner who had been fatally injured, in one of the neighboring mines, was brought in. All the cots in the hospital were filled with patients at the time, and Dr. Walters, who was a German, and a Jew, I believe, was a very choleric man. He lost his temper on seeing the terribly injured miner laid on the floor by the friends who had brought him in. Turning to me he said, "You may go home." Miss McDonnell, the matron, stepped forward and protested against the order, declaring, "That man is not in a condition to leave the hospital." The doctor cooled down, made me a very humble apology, but I declined to stay longer. With a generosity wholly unexpected, he came in his private carriage and drove me to the depot himself.

Having caught cold in the wound after the operation I was a very sick man, and should not have left the hospital for two or three weeks; but my blood boiled at the unspeakable meanness of the doctor. He had charged me one hundred dollars, and exacted payment in advance of performing the operation; whereas Dr. Smith had charged but ten dollars, and nothing at all for the second operation.

I stayed all night in Wheeling, which was then the capital of the new state of West Virginia. In the hotel there were several members of the legislature who seemed to be well-to-do farmers. I was in the uniform of a private, and the stench from my wound attracted their attention.[158] I removed the bandage and showed them where I had been operated on. The surgeon's knife had made two deep gashes in my side, which being aggravated by the cold were dreadful and sickening to look at. They assured me that the government would take care of its brave defenders, and they treated me with marked consideration until I retired for the night, which I spent in great pain.

Next morning I resumed the homeward journey, returning to Piedmont on the Baltimore & Ohio railroad; thence up George's creek to the Borden Shaft, two miles from home, where being feverish and in pain I rested for the night. I was taken home in the morning in a very emaciated condition. When my mother met me she exclaimed: "Oh, he is dying."

Dr. Smith's two operations did not weaken me much; but the incisions of Dr. Walters were exceedingly painful and exhausting, and were aggravated by the cold in the wound, which I had contracted on my way home. I was compelled to keep my bed for two weeks, suffering more than I did when I was shot down on the battlefield.

Dr. Porter called and gave me a good scolding for not consulting him before going to Pittsburgh, and denounced Dr. Walters for butchering me the way he had, and for ordering me to return home before I was in condition to travel. He insisted that I had a right to remain until I had so far recovered from the operation, as to be able to travel with safety, even though it took two months or longer.

I grew weaker every day; I could not turn in bed, and began to despair of recovery. My friends who called to see me also began to lose hope. All at once, after ten days of terrible suffering, the pain in the wound began to dry up, and in ten days or two weeks more disappeared altogether.[159]

After I got well I was discharged from the army for physical disability and placed on the pension roll at six dollars a month; in a short time it was increased to eight dollars, then to a full pension.[160] After the war closed, Congress enacted a law increasing the rate, and I am now receiving twenty-four dollars a month.

All the pieces of bone extracted from my wound were placed in a box and kept as a war relic. In 1874 my wife was showing them to some lady visitors and then put the box on the mantel-piece. The hired girl, in cleaning the room, unconscious of the contents of the box, threw it in the fire; and thus perished a war relic which money could not have purchased.[161]

HERE ENDS ROY'S MEMOIR

Afterword

J UNE 1863 SAW the Civil War reaching its climax. On the fifteenth, Confederate troops crossed the Potomac River from Virginia and invaded the North. Before the end of the month Robert E.
Lee's Army of Northern Virginia would be roaming unchecked across
Maryland and Pennsylvania, and the fortunes of the North's war effort
would reach its lowest ebb. Andrew Roy's former comrades in the
Pennsylvania Reserves were among those marching through the summer
heat in pursuit of the invaders, and many in both armies believed that the
outcome of the next battle would determine the result of the war.

By the time the armies converged at the crossroads town of Gettysburg,
Pennsylvania, on July 1, Roy had already reached and passed his personal
crossroad. He had survived his wound and was growing stronger; the
great crisis had passed but the road ahead was cast in shadows.

Two things became clear to the army with respect to Andrew Roy
that summer. First, he was improving and would no longer need regular
attention by government physicians. Second, he would never again be of
any use on a battle line. According to Dr. J. B. Lewis, at the Clarysville
Hospital, Roy was ". . . incapable of performing the duties of a soldier
because of gunshot wounds of the hip producing fracture of the left iliac
bone. . . . Disability total." The army's logic was ruthlessly simple: If the
man could not soldier, the army was no place for him. On June 13, 1862,
the war department unburdened itself of one liability and gave Private
Andrew Roy a medical discharge. He was no longer an army problem.

"Disability total," as Dr. Lewis had phrased it, meant Roy was
unable to perform the hard labor of coal mining. At times he could barely
walk. Though his discharge gave him more freedom it took from him the

pay, clothing, rations and medical care due a soldier. So while his Army of the Potomac moved through Maryland toward destiny at Gettysburg, Roy was limped alone toward an uncertain future.

He found a job weighing coal at a mine near his home in Frostburg, but he must have known at this early stage of his recovery that he would need assistance from the government. As a wounded veteran, he was entitled to a pension, and in September 1863, he applied for benefits. The doctor who examined him, the first of many who would poke and prod that ravaged abdomen in the next four and a half decades, recorded that ". . . upwards of fifty pieces of necrosis bone have been taken out of the wound and it is still open through and through and regularly discharges matter." Roy declared he was "totally disabled . . . from earning his subsistence at his regular occupation."[162]

The government demurred, however, and decreed in November 1863 that Roy was not the total wreck he claimed to be. He was, by Washington's reckoning, only three-fourths disabled. Roy was doubtless not flattered to know that the government considered him one-quarter of the man he used to be, but he nevertheless accepted the pension proffered him — six dollars per month, which was less than half his pay as a private. Out of that monthly stipend, Roy would have to pay all his expenses, including medical bills. Convinced he was entitled to, and in need of more, Roy petitioned for an increase in the pension, thereby initiating a loveless correspondence with bureaucratic Washington that would endure for nearly fifty years.

Dr. C. H. Ohr, of Cumberland, Maryland, examined Roy in April 1864, twenty-two months after Gaines's Mill, and described what he found:

> Gunshot wound entering the abdomen one inch in front of the anterior superior spinous process of the left Iliac bone passing out on the posterior surface midway between the spinal column and the anterior spine of the Ilium two inches above the hip joint. The destruction of bone and muscles covering the bone has so far destroyed the action of the hip joint as to prevent the throwing of the leg outward from the body.

Roy's pelvis had been wrecked on the left side, and he had difficulty walking. Despite the obvious severity of the wound, Roy could not convince the government to take any action on his claim for a larger pension until March 1868. Unfortunately, Washington's response was less than satisfactory: The government *reduced* his pension to four dollars per month and rated his disability at half. By government standards, Roy was healing nicely.

The first five years after his release from the army saw great changes in Roy's life. He had met Janet Watson six months after his discharge and married her seven months after that. She gave birth to their first child, Maggie, in October 1865 and was pregnant with their second when the pension bureau reduced their benefits. The family finally left Frostburg and moved to Churchill, Ohio, near Youngstown. There, Roy renewed his assault on Washington, telling doctors in 1872 that "while walking rapidly or for any length of time or while working (particularly lifting anything of weight) the whole left leg becomes weak and sore and the wound itself is now frequently quite painful."

Roy continued working in mining, but, perhaps out of necessity, devoted himself to learning the less physically taxing side of the business. He learned about mine administration and safety, and his schooling and his writing ability began to help him. He made such a name for himself in the industry that the governor of Ohio appointed him to a commission consider mine safety in the state. Roy's report impressed the state legislature and led to the creation of a state office for mine oversight. Roy became Ohio's first state mine inspector in 1871 and would hold the post until 1879. Roy apparently felt comfortable in the public arena, for in 1875 he ran for secretary of state of Ohio. He lost, and thereafter gave himself to business more than politics.

More than fifteen years after the bullet hit him and carried away part of his pelvis, Roy still suffered pain and disability. "There is weakness in left limb [leg]," he told a doctor in 1878, "and during the past eighteen months severe pain at times in the region of wound, particularly after prolonged labor." Roy said he had to "quit work at three different periods during the past twelve months from pain of wound [and] at one time was idle for five weeks, by reason of [the] wound hurting. Weakness & pain are getting worse." The pension bureau bent slightly before Roy's onslaught and modestly increased his monthly benefits to eight dollars.

The Roy family included five children, aged thirteen to newborn, when in 1878 Andrew purchased 125 acres in southern Ohio west of the town of Wellston. Other families settled nearby and the village that sprang up came to be called Glen Roy after its most prominent family. The leader of the clan stayed busy, serving as a member of state geological survey and traveling extensively to consult for coal mining companies as far away as Texas and Mexico. Roy helped develop a geological curriculum at Ohio State University and wrote extensively for mining and geological journals in America and England. He published three books on mining in addition to his war memoir. He was, by the 1880s, recognized as perhaps the leading authority on Ohio's mineral resources.

The twentieth anniversary of Roy's parole from Confederate captivity was marked by the birth of his seventh and last child, James. But in addition to the joys of his large family, Roy still had the unwelcome companionship of pain and weakness in his left leg. His pension continued to rise as Congress authorized ever more liberal allowances to disabled veterans, but Roy sincerely believed his suffering entitled him to more. "All the money I have ever received from the Government as a pensioner," he wrote to a bureaucrat, "is less than I lost. . . . I have never been without pain a single moment, since the wound healed up."[163]

Roy continued to work through the 1880s and 1890s and, in company with hundreds of thousands of other veterans, widows and orphans, relentlessly laid siege to the pension bureau. As he got older, his leg bothered him more. By 1902, he was limping badly and was at times unable to walk at all. Government doctors considering his incessant requests for more pension could find no evidence of "vicious habits," but Roy's robust constitution clearly began to weaken. Around the turn of the century, he carried 197 pounds on his five-foot eight-inch frame and had been described as "obese." Five years later, he was fifteen pounds lighter and by 1912 he had wasted to the point that a doctor described him as "poorly nourished . . . nervous, and . . . decrepit." He weighed less than 170 pounds.

"My lameness grows worse and pain is more severe each year," Roy wrote. "My foot seems dead." His leg went numb for long periods, and pressure on either of his wounds sent pain shooting through his thigh and calf. The muscles in the hip, leg and foot atrophied, causing the leg to frequently give way, and he bore bruises from frequent falls. A surgeon finally declared "This claimant is so disabled from gunshot wound of left iliac bone as to be incapacitated in a degree equivalent to loss of a hand or foot for the purposes of manual labor and is entitled to $24.00 a month."

By January 1912, seventy-seven-year-old Roy was out of work and could walk only with the assistance of a long heavy cane, on which he supported himself with both hands. He needed help in getting dressed and could not leave the house alone.[164] More than a year before Roy's death, a doctor recorded that Roy was "wholly unfit to care for himself and demands a constant attendant."[165]

The end came at last for Roy on October 19, 1914. He died at home at the age of eighty and was buried two days later in Glen Roy Cemetery. All of Roy's surviving children and grandchildren were present as he was laid to rest beside his mother, his brother, and his son, David Tod Roy, who had died ten years earlier.[166] One neighbor marked the veteran's passing with a small tribute: "He was a gentleman of culture, . . .and his life was an exemplification of the accomplishments attainable by those who cultivate their natural genius and grasp their opportunities."[167]

It says much about the age in which he lived that Roy's life was considered exemplary but not necessarily extraordinary, at least not with respect to his fifty-two-year struggle against physical disability. He was a man of his time, merely one among the scarred hundreds of thousands who soldiered on against the legacy of an unhappy instant in their youth when a piece of hurtling metal redirected their lives. If there was anything exceptional about Private Roy it might have been the philosophical cheerfulness with which he seemed to bear his cross. Buttressed by the wisdom of poets and the lessons of history, he limped onward, dauntless in the knowledge that "The mind is its own place and in itself can make a heaven of hell and a hell of heaven."

If he reflected on the path that took him on that summer evening to the fateful spot in the Virginia forest, Roy looked back with neither anger nor self-pity. Four years before his death, he contemplated his twenty-four months in the army, weighed it against half a century of pain, and wrote, "I have never regretted this part of my life, and would do it again."[170]

Medical Commentary
on the Case of Andrew Roy

By Clyde B. Kernek, M.D.

T HIS IS A different kind of Civil War account. It is not about
great fighting units, great leaders, glorious victories, crushing
defeats or legendary feats of bravery. This is the rest of the story
— the real war at the human level. This is one man's personal record of
trepidation, pain, hope and joy. It is the story of the lowly private and the
spirit of risk-takers. Multiply this tale by hundreds of thousands, and we
may be able to touch the humanity of history and begin to understand
what those Americans of the 1860s saw, felt, endured and gave to us.

The Wound, June 27, 1862

Andrew Roy was a healthy twenty-seven-year-old man when a bullet
struck him in the left groin and passed through his pelvis. If it was like
most bullets of the Civil War, the one that hit Roy weighed about an
ounce and was made of soft lead that deformed on impact, making it
capable of doing great damage to soft tissues. Rifle-muskets of the period
had a muzzle velocity of about nine hundred feet per second, giving the
balls enough energy to fracture bone. This was a high-tech weapon at
that time, accurate and powerful enough to be deadly or inflict severe
wounds on its victims. Wounds in the extremities were frequently severe,
and surgeons often sought to manage them by amputating the affected
limb. Wounds to the head, chest, and abdomen were often fatal.

The entrance wound of the minié ball was near the anterior superior
iliac spine (front) of the ilium (bone) of Roy's pelvis. As it entered Roy's

body, the bullet probably injured the lateral femoral cutaneous nerve causing numbness of the lateral (outer) thigh. The inguinal ligament and the thin abdominal wall muscles in this area would have been penetrated, and injury to the deep circumflex iliac vessels could have been a source of bleeding. Next, as the bullet neared the bone of the ilium, it would have penetrated the iliacus muscle and shattered the ilium, making this injury an open (compound) comminuted (multiple fragments of bone) fracture of the ilium. Some of the shattered bony fragments would become necrotic (dead) bone, and with the bacterial contamination and the nonviable injured tissues, the wound would become infected. If the patient survived the acute infection, he was at risk for chronic infection of the wound, including chronic osteomyelitis (inflammation of bone) of the ilium. The pieces of infected, dead bone would become sequestra, and would have to be removed before the drainage of pus would cease and the wound could heal.

Roy's abdominal cavity and bowel were apparently not injured, which was a close call, for injury to the intestines would most likely have been mortal. After the bullet crashed through the wing of the ilium, it next penetrated the abductor muscles for the hip. The now-deformed lead ball, which might have broken into fragments, penetrated and severely lacerated the gluteus medius and gluteus minimus muscles. The bullet might have injured the superior gluteal artery and vein, which would have caused considerable bleeding into the wound cavity. The superior gluteal nerve may have been injured, paralyzing the tensor fasciae latae muscle as well as the gluteus medius and minimus. The patient would have little or no active abduction of the hip, and this would cause a considerable limp requiring a cane to help him walk. Next, the bullet and fragments of lead and bone would penetrate the gluteus maximus muscle before exiting the skin a few inches proximal (above) and posterior (behind) the greater trochanter of the femur (hip). This is the exit wound, and most of the bullet would have exited from the body, but small lead fragments might have remained behind in the wound tract. The projectile might have carried cloth from Roy's uniform into the body, some of which might have remained in the wound, further contributing to the infection problem. Small lead fragments in the soft tissues would probably not pose a problem. Fortunately, the bullet did not injure the hip joint.

Private Roy had sustained a gunshot wound to the left side of his pelvis with an open, comminuted fracture of the left ilium with severe injury to his hip abductor muscles. If he survived the acute bleeding and the inevitable infection of his minié ball wound, he would face possible chronic infection and osteomyelitis of his ilium and chronic purulent drainage complicated by retained necrotic (dead) bone fragments. Even if he cleared his infection and healed his wounds, he would be faced with loss of active abduction of his left hip and a permanent limp.

Treatment Of Injury

Stretcher bearers carried Roy to an ambulance wagon, which transported him to the regimental field hospital. The assistant surgeon, Dr. McKinney, gave him liquor (a depressant), which physicians considered a treatment for shock. His wounds were washed with water (not sterile), and a surgeon or hospital steward applied dressings (not sterile). McKinney thought it was lucky "that the ball came out where it did." He may have recognized that this was not necessarily a mortal wound, if the bowel was uninjured. And so the doctor probably thought that Roy had gotten lucky that afternoon, as there was a chance that the bullet had not perforated his gut. How could he know?

But Private Roy overheard the regimental surgeon imply to Captain Adams that his wound was mortal. The surgeon probably assumed that Roy's bowel must have been injured. That night the wound became inflamed and very painful.

The next day, the Confederates captured Roy because he could not withdraw with the Federal army. His pain eased, and he was able to drink coffee and eat hard tack, which suggests that the wound indeed did not involve his abdominal cavity and bowel. The Confederates carried him by stretcher to a house and placed him on the ground under a shade tree. This became his hospital for the next sixteen days.

A Confederate surgeon washed the blood from his entrance and exit wounds and proclaimed this wound mortal, apparently because he thought it deep and likely to involve the gut. Had the bullet so much as nicked the bowel, Roy might well have died in three days from peritonitis. Field surgeons quickly examined the wounded, decided which had mortal wounds, and directed those who could not be saved to be moved out of the way to die while they worked on those they thought had a chance to live. But these surgeons had few diagnostic aids, and some of the men with "mortal wounds" survived. The doctors had no imaging studies such as X-rays (Roentgenograms [X-rays] were discovered thirty years after the Civil War), so it is no wonder that they could not accurately diagnose the extent of gunshot wounds or fractures.

The Confederate surgeon left Roy to die, so Roy had to take care of himself. He had no bandages so probably reused his soiled, contaminated dressing or made new ones from clothing. He used water to keep the dressings wet and to cool the heat of the inflammatory response about his large wound, but neither the dressings nor the water were sterile. Further, it appears Roy endured all of his pain without relief from medication.

As Roy lost blood, he became weak and thirsty. When raised to a sitting position, he felt faint from hypotension. A few days later he began to gain strength and was able to crawl and regain some mobility. Since he could drink fluids and eat food, he gradually started to recover. The key was that his intestines were uninjured and functioning. Private Roy had a chance to survive, if his natural immune system could contain the inevitable acute infection to the area of the wound.

In the summer heat, maggots filled his wounds. Comrades tried to clean out the maggots and applied turpentine to his wounds, but turpentine is harsh on tissues. The well-meaning friends would have done better to leave the maggots alone as the creatures would have helped to clean the wounds by eating dead tissue. Still, Roy's condition improved in the fresh air outside on the ground under his shade tree. After more than two weeks, he was transferred to Richmond and was able to limp from the train depot to the prison. The prison building was much worse for Roy than the ground under the shade tree had been. He had to lie on a filthy floor infested with lice, breathe foul air that irritated his lungs, and eat poor rations.

His wounds drained copious amounts of pus, known as "laudable pus." Surgeons considered laudable pus a sign that the wound was healing. Roy reused his shirt as a dressing by washing it and his wounds in a common water tank used by other wounded men as well. The water in the tank became contaminated, but bacteriology was unknown to these men and their doctors.

Fortunately for Roy, the Confederates soon paroled him. He was able to walk from the prison to the train, a good sign that he was recovering from his wound. His immune system had controlled the infection and spared him from septicemia (blood poisoning), which would have been fatal. He had apparently inherited a rugged constitution with a good natural resistance to infection, and he never lost hope.

At the Union hospital at Fort Monroe, the surgeons thought his wounds would heal in a few months — but this was not to be. Roy had developed chronic osteomyelitis of the left ilium with necrotic (dead) bone. His wounds would continue to drain pus as long as the necrotic bone remained within him. At the General Hospital at Annapolis, Maryland, a surgeon inserted a probe (not sterile) in the exit wound until it passed through the hole in the ilium. The surgeons, of course, didn't know about antiseptic and aseptic techniques. The surgeon diagnosed necrotic (dead) bone and commented that what saved Roy's life was that his bowels were not injured. He thought that several months would be needed for the wounds to stop draining pus and decompose the dead bone. Sequestra of dead bone would either spit out of the wound or continue as a source of chronic osteomyelitis with purulent drainage. Roy needed a surgical operation to remove the necrotic bone so that his wound would heal, but this surgeon thought that a surgical procedure to remove the dead bone was too risky and that the patient would surely die. This opinion was realistic at that time because surgery to remove dead bone from the ilium could cause severe bleeding and spread the infection into other tissue planes with fatal results. Any injury to the bowel would surely have been fatal.

Roy's wounds continued to drain, and some small pieces of dead bone spit out of the exit wound. The surgeon finally realized that all of the dead bone would need to be extruded from the wound before recovery would be complete and the drainage cease.

In December 1862, the Army transferred Roy to the General Hospital at Clarysville, Maryland. The surgeon there, Dr. Townsend, irrigated the wound with warm soapy water, which was a good idea because the soap would have some antiseptic effect, although Dr. Townsend would not have known about bacteriology. The entrance and exit wounds were connected by a tract so the irrigation fluid would traverse the wound. Dr. Townsend recognized it was a miracle that the bowels were not injured by the bullet. Meanwhile, the wounds continued to drain pus.

By the summer of 1863, Roy was still being treated at the General Hospital at Clarysville, and the surgeon in charge, Dr. Lewis, felt surgery to excise the dead bone was too risky. He thought the procedure would kill the patient, and told Roy to wait for nature to extrude the dead bone from the body.

Surgery by Civilian Surgeons

Andrew Roy sought a second opinion from a civilian doctor that summer of 1863. He wanted a cure. He wanted surgery to excise the necrotic bone and was willing to risk death.

Dr. Smith in Baltimore probed Roy's wound and diagnosed necrotic bone. In his efforts to remove the fragments, Smith used forceps (not sterile) in the entrance wound and pulled out 14 pieces of bone. This blind probing and manipulation of the wound without anesthesia was painful for Roy, and it was risky as well. Smith could have injured the bowel, caused major bleeding, injured a nerve and spread the infection. The patient had to be very brave, and the surgeon had to be daring.

Ten weeks later, the purulent wound drainage was the same as before surgery. Dr. Smith operated again and removed by forceps only one small piece of necrotic bone. He thought that he had removed all of the dead bone.

The wounds were still draining in the autumn of 1863, so Roy got another opinion. Dr. Walter of Pittsburgh probed the wound, but he did not think there was any more necrotic bone. He did suspect a foreign body such as cloth from Roy's uniform. Dr. Walter made incisions to enlarge the entrance and exit wounds and probed the wound tract through the ilium by inserting each bare middle finger (not sterile) in each wound until the finger tips touched. Fingers made good probes, but the procedure must have been very painful without anesthesia (Roy took pain medicine after the operation). Dr. Walter used forceps to pull out a large piece of necrotic bone, and then another, and one wonders if these blind procedures to pull bone from the wounds could have damaged the abductor muscles or the superior gluteal nerve even beyond the damage the bullet had caused.

After this painful procedure, the wound became more inflamed, and Roy became very ill from infection. He was in bed two weeks, and then the drainage decreased. He steadily improved so that by October or

November 1863 the drainage stopped, and the wound healed.

Roy's Disability

Once his wounds had healed in late winter 1863, Roy's permanent impairment was his limp. With iliac bone missing and direct injury to the gluteus medius and minimus muscles, and the probable injury to the superior gluteal nerve, Roy lost active abduction of his left hip causing a significant limp. This limp would be an abductor lurch (Trendelenburg gait), in which the patient shifts his center of gravity toward the weak hip. A cane in his right hand would help his gait, but Roy was able to walk without a cane.

In 1902, forty years after his injury, Roy complained of chronic pain, weakness, and numbness. Pressure on either the entrance or exit wound scars caused shooting pain through his thigh and calf. The entrance wound scar would have involved the lateral femoral cutaneous nerve and would explain this pain in the lateral thigh. But the exit wound was not near nerves that would radiate into the calf. Perhaps Roy had developed a low back problem that radiated pain into his calf.

The Surgeon's Certificate of 1907 [*see* page 106] reported the "Considerable wasting" of the left gluteal muscles, confirming the severe injury to the abductor muscles of the hip. This also supports the possibility of superior gluteal nerve injury and paralysis of the hip abductors.

By 1912, fifty years after injury, the seventy-seven-year-old Roy could walk only with a cane. A year later, an examining physician gave the opinion that the sciatic nerve was involved by scar tissue. As the wound tract was not near the sciatic nerve, it is unclear how scar tissue would involve the sciatic nerve, unless the infection had spread to the nerve and caused scarring about it.

Roy died in 1914, at eighty years of age. He had survived his gunshot wound by fifty-two years, a far cry from the three days predicted by the Confederate surgeon. In his last few decades of life, he may have developed arthritis of the left hip, which would have added to the disability of weak hip abductor muscles. Whether he had causalgia (reflex sympathetic dystrophy) as a cause of chronic pain in the left lower extremity, we will never know.

Despite Roy's physical impairment — his limp and pain in the left

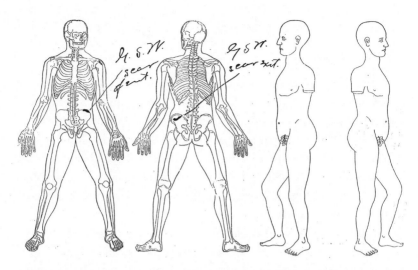

Like millions of veterans, North and South, Roy applied for a government pension after the war and thereby subjected himself to frequent
and extensive physical examinations. The Surgeon's Certificate (above
and on facing page) records some observations on Roy by an examining
board of three physicians in 1907. The abbreviation "G.S.W." stands
for gunshot wound.

hip, he functioned fairly well for several decades. He married and raised
a family, was gainfully employed, traveled extensively, and published
books. Roy overcame his physical disability because he used his mind —
"The mind is its own place and in itself can make a heaven of hell. . . ."

A Modern Perspective

Modern treatment of Roy's wound would be aggressive. Shock
would be treated by intravenous fluids and blood replacement as needed.
Medical personnel would dispense pain medicine, and bandages would
be sterile. He would be evacuated from the field as soon as possible by
ambulance or helicopter and after arrival at a hospital he would be taken
to an operating room as soon as his condition was stable. Imaging studies
such as X-ray would define the fracture and help determine if bowel had
been perforated. Operating room staff would administer general anes-

SURGEON'S CERTIFICATE

IN CASE OF

Andrew Roy.

Co. *7*, *10* Reg't *Pa. Inf.*

APPLICANT FOR *Inc.*

No. *27.311*

DATE OF EXAMINATION:

Apr 3rd, 190 *7*

J. B. Galvin, Pres.,
W. P. Evans, Sec'y, } BOARD.
G. Darling, Treas.,

Post office, *Jackson.*

County, *Jackson.*

State, *Ohio.*

Do not use backs of certificates for any purpose other than indicated by printed matter thereon.   6—862b

Witnesses to mark: {

(Signature of Applicant.)

"I, —— the applicant for (increase or original) pension referred to in this medical certificate, hereby consent to be examined by Dr. —— and Dr. ——, the examining surgeons here present (waiving examination by full board), on this —— day of ——, 190 ."

(This certificate to be filled in by the member of the board acting as secretary, and signed by the applicant, when a full board is not present.)

(Signature.)

of ——, 190 *7*

examination of *Andrew Roy*, the claimant in this case, on —— day

Dr. ——, were personally present and actually participated in the

"I hereby certify that Dr. ——, Dr. ——, and

W. P. Evans,

An examination must not be made by one member of a board except upon a special order of the Commissioner of Pensions.

(This certificate to be filled in and signed by the secretary when the full board is present.)

thesia, and a surgeon — under sterile conditions — would debride his wounds to excise all damaged and nonviable soft tissues and bone. Intravenous antibiotics would help prevent and treat infection. Staged surgery would be done for delayed primary closure to close the wound and allow it to heal without infection. If infection developed, it would be treated aggressively with surgical debridement and intravenous antibiotics. Cultures of the bacteria would allow staff members to select the most effective antibiotics.

Under modern management, Roy's gunshot wound most likely would heal in a few weeks without infection. He would undergo rehabilitation to strengthen active abductor muscles, if there was any function remaining. He might also receive training for a lighter job than coal mining.

But what about Roy's modern long-term outcome? His hip abductors would still be weak or possibly unable to actively abduct his hip, so he would still walk with a limp and use a cane. Thus, the long-term outcome in Roy's case would probably be about the same with modern treatment as it really was for him. The chief difference modern medicine would have made is that if his bowel had been perforated, he most likely would have died in 1862, while with modern treatment he probably would survive a bowel injury.

It is not quite fair for us to judge medicine and surgery of the Civil War. We were not there, and we cannot erase our knowledge of bacteriology and all the other advances in medicine so that we might view medical problems as did surgeons of the day. We should only judge them in the context of their own time and not ours. In their time, they performed their duties as well as we could have had we been in their place.

Appendix 1:

Ordering of Chapters

To focus Roy's narrative more sharply on the compelling story of his struggle with his wounds, I slightly reorganized his chapters (see concluding section in Preface, beginning page 11). All chapter titles were retained, but the chapters in Roy's original manuscript have been renumbered as follows:

current chapter number : *original chapter number*

1	:	2
2	:	3
3	:	4
4	:	5
5	:	6
6	:	7
7	:	8
8	:	9
9	:	10
10	:	11
11	:	12
12	:	14
13	:	15
14	:	16
15	:	17
16	:	18
17	:	19
18	:	20
App. 3	:	13
App. 4	:	21
App. 5	:	22

Appendix 2:

Roy's Notes on the Pennsylvania Reserves

The Pennsylvania Reserve Volunteer Corps, as it was officially known, included men from all over Pennsylvania and some neighboring states. These soldiers enjoyed an unusually high sense of esprit de corps. Roy was typical in his pride of having belonged to the Reserves, and in the first chapter of his book he included the following description (annotations added by the editor).

"[The Pennsylvania Reserve Volunteer Corps] consisted of thirteen regiments of infantry, one regiment of cavalry and several batteries of artillery.

The division, which was commanded by Major General George A. McCall, was divided into three brigades: the first being commanded by Brigadier General John F. Reynolds, the second by Brigadier General George G. Meade, the third by Brigadier General E. O. C. Ord.[169] The Pennsylvania Reserves was the only division in the Union Army in which all the regiments were from the same state.

These three brigade commanders rose to high command: General Meade to the command of the Army of the Potomac; General Reynolds to the command of the First Corps in the Army of the Potomac (he was killed in the Battle of Gettysburg, July 1, 1863); General Ord to the command of a corps in the Army of the Potomac. The presence of the Pennsylvania Reserves in Washington, the day after the First Battle of Bull Run, saved the capital from being captured by the enemy.[170]

The division was in eighteen battles. Of the forty-seven regiments which sustained the greatest losses in battle, during the war, forty belonged to the Army of the Potomac, eleven of which were Pennsylvania regiments, four of them being regiments of the Pennsylvania Reserve Volunteer Corps, and one of the four was the Tenth. In the assault of the

Union Army at Fredericksburg the Reserves lost, in killed and wounded, more men than Pickett's division at the Battle of Gettysburg.

The Reserves went into action at Fredericksburg with an effective force of 4,475 men, and lost as follows:

Killed	Wounded	Missing	Total
175	1,241	457	1,873
3.9%	27%	9.7%	41.3%

Pickett's division went into battle at Gettysburg with an effective force of 6,204 men, and lost as follows:

Killed	Wounded	Missing	Total
232	1,157	1,499	2,888
3.7%	18.6 %	24.1%	46.4% [171]

Appendix 3:

Roy's Notes on Southern Unionists

Roy observed Southerners with a curious detachment and willingly made generalizations about them as a people. He included this essay in his narrative as chapter 13.

Union Sentiment of the South

Although to outward appearances the South was a unit to destroy the Union, there was as a matter of fact quite a Union sentiment even in the capital of the Confederacy, which manifested itself as much as it dared in the interest of the prisoners. A lithe, little woman, evidently, judging from the plainness of her dress, the wife of a poor man, passed the prison daily and threw in a loaf of bread through a window of the lower story. She belonged to the common people, which Lincoln said "God loved, or he would not have made so many of them."[172] A single loaf of bread would not add much to the scant bill of fare of eight hundred prisoners; but the spirit which inspired the act did the prisoners more good than a thousand loaves would have done by order of the Southern Confederacy.

The common people of the South — the poor whites, as the slave-holding element called them — were loyal at heart until the mad passions of the politicians precipitated the attack on Fort Sumter. I was a citizen of Arkansas when the war broke out, and was clerk of the election of the precinct in which I resided when the convention was elected to take the state out of the Union. There were only four slave owners in the precinct, all of whom voted for the delegate who favored secession. There were forty-four votes cast altogether, and forty of them were cast for the Union candidate.

Of the sixty-five delegates elected to the state convention, thirty-five were for the Union and thirty for secession. The convention met at Little Rock, the state capital, and immediately adjourned to meet again the following August. After the bombardment of Fort Sumter it reconvened and passed the Ordinance of Secession with a whirl.

The people among whom I lived were farmers, who owned the land they tilled, and were Southerners from Kentucky, Missouri, Tennessee and Alabama. They were too poor to own slaves and hated the system as heartily as either Horace Greeley or Wendell Phillips. I boarded with James Crockett, a distant relative of the celebrated backwoodsman of Tennessee, and he possessed many of the traits of character of his uncle, the eccentric Congressman, and was a bold outspoken Union man. When the war broke out he declined to enlist, declaring that he would never shoulder a musket to aid in breaking up the government of his fathers, and insisted that no state convention, or any other state authority, had power to pass an ordinance of secession. When he was drafted he declined to report for duty, and told the provost guard who came to arrest him that they could shoot him or hang him, but he would never lift a gun against his own countrymen.

One of the lawyers of Fort Smith was also a bold, outspoken Union man, and said in public speech, before the war opened, "that if any state dared to organize a rebellion against the authority of the United States it was the duty of the general government to use coercion to compel obedience to its authority." The speech raised a storm of indignation about the lawyer's ears and he was compelled to make a recantation to save his life; but, like Galileo, he was still in favor of coercion to compel obedience to the national authority, and he lived to put his principles into practice. After the Union troops captured Fort Smith he raised a regiment of loyal Arkansasians[173] and fought for the Union. He was elected governor of the state in 1884. Being in Arkansas the same year, I called upon him in Fort Smith; he remembered me very well. After meeting the Governor I inquired of an old acquaintance of ante-bellum[174] days how it came to pass that the people of Arkansas had elected a Union Colonel Governor. "O, well," replied my friend, "he helped to reorganize the state after the war, and we forgave him."[175]

Appendix 4:

Roy's Winter on the Rio Grande

Around the turn of the century, Roy lived in Minera, Texas, for three months to attend to business with the operators of nearby coal mining operations. He recorded many observations and opinions of the Mexicans and the country along the Rio Grande, and, strangely, he decided to make his notes on the trip part of his war memoir. He made this the penultimate chapter in his book, but because it is long, slightly incoherent and completely out of character with the rest of Roy's book, the chapter is better briefly summarized than presented verbatim.

Roy confidently declared that Mexicans were an inferior race because they were "not a brave and aggressive people like the Americans" and remarked upon such diverse subjects as Spanish courting customs, class divisions, the educational system in Texas, the Mexican method of making cornbread, the climate in southwest Texas, a celebration in honor of Washington's birthday, bull fights and beautiful women. Not surprisingly, Roy expressed opinions about many of the things he saw, frequently making generalizations about the Mexican people and their society based on his observations of specific instances.

The most interesting anecdote in Roy's story of his trip to Texas comes in the final paragraph of the chapter. Roy wrote:

While walking one day I was introduced to a Southern soldier; a splendid specimen of the Johnny Reb. We soon drifted into a discussion of the Civil War, and found that we had both been in the battle of Gaines's Mill, on opposite sides, and both been very severely wounded in the battle. I told him that I had witnessed a splendid charge on one of our batteries. "Well," said he, "I was wounded in that charge." He lived in San Antonio, but was visiting his sister at Lerido.[176] When he went for dinner he told his sister that he had met the Yankee who shot him, but he had shot the Yankee worse than he had shot him.

Appendix 5:

Roy's Recollections of Abraham Lincoln

The final chapter in the 1909 edition of Roy's book was derived from a speech he delivered in Wellston, Ohio, February 14, 1909, to mark the one hundredth anniversary of Abraham Lincoln's birth. Though the chapter has nothing to do with Roy's personal experiences during the war, it is included here in its entirety because it contains morsels of information about his life prior to the war.

The Lincoln-Douglas Debate — Lincoln Reviews the Army of the Potomac

Shortly after Illinois was admitted into the Union two young men settled in the wooden capital of the new state. One came from Kentucky, the other from Vermont; one was a common rail-splitter, the other a common carpenter. Abraham Lincoln was the name of the rail-splitter, Stephen Arnold Douglas the name of the carpenter. Nature had stamped her signet mark of genius on the foreheads of both. Douglas developed early. He was a member of the United States Senate at thirty-three. In those days there were giants in the Senate, but Douglas soon forged to the front and held his own with the best.

Slavery had been a disturbing element since the formation of the Union. The Missouri Compromise, which was enacted in 1820 prohibited it in the Territories forever; and it was now believed that it never would again disturb the public mind. A subsequent decision of the Supreme Court, however, was handed down by Chief Justice Tawny [Taney], which declared the Missouri Compromise unconstitutional; and Senator Douglas soon afterward introduced a bill in the Senate for the abrogation of the law.

The Slavery agitation now burst out anew with intensified fury. A new party was organized in every Northern state, composed of old line Whigs, Free Soil Democrats and Abolitionists, to replace the Whig party, which had been beaten to a frazzle.

Abraham Lincoln, who had been a rail-splitter, a flat-boatman, a country storekeeper, a local post-master, a land surveyor, a member of the state legislature, and had served one term in Congress, was nominated by the new party for United States Senator against Douglas, who had recently been nominated by the Democrats for a third term. In his speech accepting the nomination, Lincoln uttered the following prophetic words:

"A house divided against itself cannot stand. I believe that this government cannot exist half slave and half free. I do not expect the Union to be dissolved; I do not expect the house to fall; but I do expect that it will cease to be divided. It will become all one thing or all the other. Either the opponents of slavery will arrest its further spread, and place it where the public mind shall rest in the belief that it is in course of ultimate extinction, or its advocates will push it forward till it shall become alike lawful in all the states — old as well as new, north as well as south."

Lincoln soon after his nomination challenged Douglas to a joint debate on the issues of the campaign. The challenge irritated Douglas. He was the leader of his party, and had a national reputation; while Lincoln was comparatively unknown outside the state of Illinois. "But," said Douglas, "I will have to accept the challenge, for Lincoln is the nominee of his party for my place in the United States Senate." How little did Douglas know that in less than two and a half years Lincoln would be standing on the portico of the Capitol reading his inaugural address as president of the United States, and at his death bequeath to his countrymen a name as the greatest American since the foundation of the government, not excepting Washington himself.

Seven debates were arranged. I was working in a coal mine near Galesburg when the fifth debate occurred, and rode up to the town on the same train which carried Douglas.

The debate took place in the Knox College grounds. The number of people present was estimated at twenty thousand. The surrounding towns and villages turned out en masse. Farmers came in their wagons,

At age 74, Roy posed for this photograph on the occasion of his 1909 address on Abraham Lincoln. Roy stood as a symbol of his generation. Hundreds of thousands were crippled by the war or suffered from chronic illness, but only a small fraction of the war-handicapped were visibly maimed. This seemingly healthy man had been limping heavily and enduring pain for more than forty years.

bringing their wives, their sons and daughters, in rain and storm, for twenty miles round about, to witness the great intellectual encounter between the two greatest orators in the state, if not in the nation.

Douglas led in the discussion in an hour's speech; Lincoln followed with an hour and a half, Douglas closing with a half hour. The seven debates were very largely a repetition of each other. Douglas began his address with a defense of the repeal of the Missouri Compromise, and then expounded what he called his great principle of Popular Sovereignty, which conferred the right of all the people to take their property into every territory of the United States, subject to no other limitation than what the Constitution imposes. In the formation of a new state he said he did not care whether slavery was voted up or voted down. The political principles which he stood for were national in character. The speech he was now making he could deliver in any state of the Union; whereas Mr. Lincoln would not dare to deliver the speech he will make today in any Southern state, for as soon as he approached the Ohio River he would find the people on the other side shaking their fists in his face.

Douglas insisted that Negroes were not included in the Declaration of Independence, and that it was a slander to even suppose that negroes were meant to be included in it. He called Lincoln an abolitionist, and that he wanted to marry a "nigger" wife. He charged Lincoln with having assisted in passing a set of abolition resolutions at a Republican meeting in Springfield in 1854. He was haughty and domineering in argument. His followers called him the "Little Giant"; the Republicans called him the "Little Dodger." Both names were very appropriate.

When Lincoln rose to reply the contrast between the make-up of the two men was striking. Douglas was only five feet four inches in height. He was, however, strongly built; of handsome features and a well raised forehead. Lincoln was six feet four, lean of person and uncouth of form. His clothes hung awkwardly on his gigantic frame; his features were exceedingly homely; he had large hands and feet. But in all the virtues which men admire, and which the religion of Jesus Christ inculcates, he surpassed any public man of his time. He was honor and honesty impersonified. When he began to speak he was diffident and hesitating; but as he warmed up, he became self-reliant. He made few gestures and never moved his feet nor posed. When he wished to clinch a statement he bent his body backward and forward, and shook his massive head. When he described the wrong and wickedness of human slavery he raised his right arm aloft and brought it down with tremendous energy.

Answering Douglas' assertion that negroes were not included in the Declaration of Independence he defied him to show that, up till three years ago (when the exigencies of the Democratic party made it a necessity to invent the affirmation that negroes were not included in the Declaration of Independence), that Thomas Jefferson ever said so, that Washington ever said so, or that any living man ever said so. Lincoln propounded four questions to Douglas. The second one was fraught with tremendous consequences: "Can the people of a United States Territory, in any lawful manner against the wishes of any citizen of the United States, exclude slavery within its borders, prior to the formation of a state constitution?" Lincoln's friends advised him not to put the question, for Douglas would either answer yes, or straddle it, which will elect him Senator. "Well," answered Lincoln, "If he does it will enrage the South, and defeat his nomination for the presidency." "Well, where do you come in? "Oh," he replied, "I am after bigger game. I want to clip the wings of the 'Little Giant.' He has had the presidential itch for the past eight years; the battle of 1860 is worth a hundred of this." Lincoln put the question and Douglas answered as follows: "It matters not what way the Supreme Court may hereafter decide as to the abstract question whether slavery may or may not go into a territory under the constitution, the people have the lawful means to introduce or exclude it as they please; for the reason that slavery cannot exist a day or an hour anywhere unless it is supported by local police regulations."

This answer greatly pleased the Democrats of Illinois and other northern states; but it angered the South, and Douglas was denounced as having betrayed the Democratic party, by the southern "fire-eaters." The Democrats of Illinois carried the Legislature and Douglas was re-elected, although the Republicans carried the state by a majority of five thousand, if my memory serves me right. Douglas' answer split the Democratic party in two, and practically precipitated the Civil War two years later. It made Lincoln president.

Lincoln denied that he had been at the meeting which passed the abolition resolutions, and in turn charged Douglas and two associates with having concocted them. "And yet," exclaimed Lincoln, with great irony, "Each of the three regard each other as honorable men." While

Lincoln was charging Douglas as having forged the resolutions, Douglas took the cigar out of his mouth, turned up his face toward Lincoln, scorn and anger overspreading it.

When Douglas rose to reply he was greeted with tumultuous cheers, and it was fully five minutes before he could be heard. "My friends," he exclaimed, "the highest compliment you can pay me during the brief half hour that is left to address you is not to cheer. I want every moment of my time to reply to Abraham Lincoln."

He angrily denied that he had forged the resolutions, and declared that he would not have believed till this day that Abraham Lincoln would have said what he had said this hour. "Does Lincoln," he exclaimed, with indignation, "wish to push this thing to the point of personal quarrel?"

It turned out that both were wrong. It was an abolition meeting, and a very small one, that passed the resolutions which Douglas read, Lincoln was not at the meeting and knew nothing about them. Douglas was under the impression that the resolutions were passed at a Republican meeting, and that Lincoln had assisted in having them adopted.

During the intervals between the joint debates both candidates addressed meetings, but at different places. At one of these gatherings, Douglas (who had been indulging in the flowing bowl with a number of friends before the meeting), called Lincoln a liar and a sneak, and threatened to call him to account on the field of honor. A man in the crowd, more fuddled than Douglas, took off his coat and offered to take the job off his hands, and lick Lincoln, himself. Lincoln addressed a Republican meeting at the same place the following day. He asked the audience if anybody heard Douglas talk of fighting him at the meeting yesterday? Cries of "Yes," came in reply. "I have been informed," added Lincoln, "that a man in the crowd, more excited than Douglas, shed his coat and threatened to whip Lincoln, himself. Did anybody hear this warlike proceeding?" Cries of "Yes" came from a score of stentorian lungs. "Well, my friends," added Lincoln, "I would not advise any of you to bet on a battle; because Douglas and I are the best of friends; he would no more think of fighting me than he would of fighting his wife, and if I can't get a fight out of Douglas, I can't get one out of his bottle-holder."

The next time I had the honor of seeing Lincoln the Civil War had burst upon the country like an avalanche. The battle of Bull Run had been fought; the president had called for five hundred thousand men to suppress the rebellion. The Army of the Potomac, a hundred and fifty thousand strong, had been so well drilled that they looked like regulars. There was to be a grand review, and the President came across the Potomac with his cabinet and representative of foreign governments. I was on guard when the troops were formed in column of division. The guards were relieved from duty with leave to go where they pleased. As soon as we stacked arms we threw our belts on the bayonets and walked down to the head of the column on the right flank. The President was in front and a little to the right on horseback. His long legs nearly touched the ground, and his stove-pipe hat was stuck on the back of his head. He was waiting on Generals Butler and Mansfield. His nose became itchy and he rubbed it with the fore-finger of his right hand with great energy but with little dignity. One of the boys in the front rank said, loud enough for the President to hear the remark: "By God, there is not enough dignity there for a President of the United States."

Generals Butler and Mansfield soon came along in a two-horse carriage, and when within fifty yards of Lincoln wheeled to the right to drive to the reviewing stand. The President roared after them, "Butler, halt," and the two generals and the President after shaking hands started down to the review stand. He appeared to be as plain and unassuming as when he had his famous debate with Senator Douglas. The guards walked down to the reviewing stand. The President and his Cabinet, and the foreign representatives and a number of ladies were on the stand. I could not keep my eyes off Simon Cameron, Secretary of War. I thought he was the finest specimen of a cultured man I had ever seen. His face was clean-cut and of an aristocratic mold; his eye was as clear and as penetrating as that of an eagle. The Secretary of State, Wm. H. Seward, was also a man of bright, intelligent features; but Cameron riveted my eyes. His brother, Colonel John Cameron, had been killed at the Battle of Bull Run the preceding summer, as wild and high the Cameron pibroch rose — the war-note of Locheil, — while leading the Seventy-ninth New York Highlanders in a charge.

General McClellan and his staff rode at the head of the column of the Army of the Potomac. The general was dressed in all the paraphernalia of his rank. Solomon in all his glory was not arrayed like him. He was a fine-looking soldier, rather short in stature, but had a well-knit frame. He wore immense army gloves, which reached up to his elbows. His hat was adorned with feathers; his belts were made of cloth of gold. His eye was bright; his forehead broad; his form and bearing the beau-ideal of a soldier. He had organized the finest army of citizen soldiers on this planet. But he did not know how to fight them — there was always a lion in his path. The real general, the modest, unassuming soldier, the man of few words but mighty deeds, came at last and hammered the life out of the rebellion.

Two months ago I stood in the rotunda of the Capitol in Washington gazing on the marble statue of Lincoln. His large feet were planted firmly on the marble pedestal. His large hands and long arms hung carelessly by his sides — reminders of the days of his youth and his poverty, when he plodded over the prairies of Illinois to split rails for a living. His shrewd, kindly eye; his massive forehead; his homely, expressive features; his towering form, bending slightly forward as when he stood half a century ago on the speakers' platform at Galesburg, Illinois, and cast his eyes over the vast multitude of men and women who had assembled from village and farm, town and city to hear the issues of the most exciting political campaign discussed since the formation of the Union, by the ablest orators in the State of Illinois. But vain was all the eloquence of the two massive statesmen. The sword alone could settle the question at issue, and it took the bloodiest war in all history to settle it.

When the mad passions of the Southern oligarchy precipitated the Civil War, Douglas threw his whole soul into the conflict for the preservation of the Union. The last speech he ever made was burning with manly eloquence in support of Lincoln's administration. "Whoever is not for the Union is against the Union; in this war there can be nothing but patriots and traitors," he exclaimed. He died three months after Lincoln's inauguration. Had he lived, Lincoln would have made him Secretary of War.

Lincoln's fame has been constantly rising since the day that the bullet of a mad assassin pierced his brain. From that day he belonged to the nations and the ages. He died that the government which the valor and genius of Washington established might live.

Washington was the father of his country, Lincoln was its savior.

Bibliography

Arnold, Denis, ed. *New Oxford Companion to Music*, 2 vols. (Oxford, 1983).

Association of Graduates, *Register of Graduates and Former Cadets of the United States Military Academy* 1802-1990 (West Point, 1990).

Barnet, Sylvan, ed., *The Complete Signet Classic Shakespeare* (New York, 1963).

Bartlett , John, *Familiar Quotations*, 15th edition, Emily Morison Beck, ed. (New York, 1980).

Bates, Samuel P., *History of Pennsylvania Volunteers, 1861-65*, 5 vols. (Harrisburg, 1869-1871).

Bradford, Margaret Boni, *Fireside Book of Folk Songs* (New York, 1947).

Dictionary of American Biography, Allen Johnson and Dumas Malone, eds., 20 vols. (New York, 1943).

Fox, William F., *Regimental Losses in the American Civil War 1861-1865* (Albany, 1898).

Heitman, Francis B., *Historical Register and Dictionary of the United States Army 1789-1903*, 2 vols. (Washington, 1903).

Hennessy, John J., *Return to Bull Run* (New York, 1992).

Hughes, Merritt Y., ed., *John Milton Complete Poems and Major Prose,* (Indianapolis, 1957).

Kaufman, Martin, Stuart Galishoff, Todd L. Savitt, eds., *Dictionary of American Medical Biography*, 2 vols. (Westport, Conn., 1984).

Massachusetts Adjutant General, *Massachusetts Soldiers, Sailors and Marines in the Civil War*, 9 vols. (Norwood, Mass., 1931).

McClellan, George B., *McClellan's Own Story* (New York, 1887).

_____, *The Civil War Papers of George B. McClellan*, Stephen W. Sears, ed. (New York, 1989).

Moore, Samuel T., Jr., *Moore's Complete Civil War Guide to Richmond* (Richmond, 1978).

Newell, Joseph Keith, ed., *"Ours": Annals of 10th Regiment Massachusetts Volunteers in the Rebellion* (Springfield, 1875).

Parker, Sandra V., *Richmond's Civil War Prisons* (Lynchburg, 1990).

Pennsylvania at Gettysburg, 2 vols. (Harrisburg, 1904).

Phisterer, Frederick, *New York in the War of the Rebellion*, 6 vols. (Albany, 1912).

Roberts, Robert B., *Encyclopedia of Historic Forts* (New York, 1988).

Roe, Alfred S., *The Tenth Regiment Massachusetts Volunteer Infantry 1861-1864* (Springfield, 1909).

Roy, Andrew, *Recollections of a Prisoner of War* (Columbus, 1909).

Scharf, J. Thomas, *History of Western Maryland*, 2 vols. (Philadelphia, 1882).

Sypher, J. R., *History of the Pennsylvania Reserve Corps* (Lancaster, 1865).

The Medical and Surgical History of the Civil War, 12 volumes (Washington, DC,).

Todd, William, *The Seventy-Ninth Highlanders New York Infantry in the War of the Rebellion 1861-1865* (Albany, 1886).

U.S. War Department, *The War of the Rebellion: The Official Records of the Union and Confederate Armies*, 128 vols. (Washington D.C., 1890-1901).

University of Pennsylvania Men in the Civil War: The Alumni Register (Philadelphia, n.d.).

Who Was Who in America, Historical Volume, 1607-1896, (Chicago, 1967).

Wilmer, L. Allison, J. H, Jarrett, George W. F. Vernon, *History and Roster of Maryland Volunteers, War of the 1861-1865*, 2 vols. (Baltimore, 1898).

Woodward, Evan, *Our Campaigns* (Philadelphia, 1865 p. 96.

The Jackson (Ohio) *Herald*

National Tribune, (Washington, D.C.)

The Trumansburg (New York) *News*

The Wellston (Ohio) *Sentinel*

Notes

Prologue: To the Battle

[1] Roy Obituary, *The Wellston* (Ohio) *Sentinel*, October 21, 1914, p. 1.

[2] Roy to J. L. Davenport, Commissioner of Pensions, April 27, 1910, Roy Pension File, National Archives, Washington, D.C.

[3] Ibid.

[4] Company A of the Tenth Pennsylvania Reserves hailed from Somerset County, Pennsylvania, while the men of Roy's Company F came largely from Butler County, north of Pittsburgh. Roy might have enlisted with Company A and been transferred to Company F at a later date, a common transaction within regiments forming in 1861. The men of Company F selected as their nickname "The Curtin Rifles" in honor of Governor Curtin. J. R. Sypher, *History of the Pennsylvania Reserve Corps* (Lancaster, 1865), p. 87. According to historian William F. Fox, "The men [of the Tenth Pennsylvania Reserves] were of more than unusual intelligence and education. Company I was recruited from students at Allegheny College in Meadville, Pa., while Company D came from Jefferson College; the other companies were composed largely of similar material, teachers and pupils serving in the ranks together." Company G included many students from Jefferson College as well. Samuel P. Bates, *History of Pennsylvania Volunteers, 1861-65*, 5 vols. (Harrisburg, 1869-1871), vol. 1, p. 813; William F. Fox, *Regimental Losses in the American Civil War 1861-1865* (Albany, 1898), pp. 259-260.

[5] On December 20, 1861, Roy's brigade fought a small battle near Dranesville, Virginia.

[6] McCall's Pennsylvanian's formed a division in the Federal First Corps commanded by Major General Irvin McDowell.

[7] For more than a month near Falmouth, Roy and the rest of the Reserves worked in labor gangs repairing bridges and the railroad between Fredericksburg and the Aquia Creek landing on the Potomac. McCall's division boarded steamers on June 13 and moved down the Rappahannock to the Chesapeake Bay then up the York and the Pamunkey Rivers, arriving at McClellan's supply base at White House Landing on June 16.

[8] In 1861, McCall's division had a paper strength of fourteen thousand (excluding cavalry). Illness and the reassignment of some of the regiments and companies reduced McCall's division to about eight thousand men present at Beaver Dam Creek in late June 1862.

[9] George W. McCracken, "Address at Dedication of Monument," *Pennsylvania at Gettysburg*, 2 vols. (Harrisburg, 1904), vol. 1, p. 264. Roy's Company F lay in support of Captain Henry V. DeHart's Battery C, Fifth U.S. Artillery for a time and this was probably the battery he refers to in the next two sentences. U.S. War

Department, *The War of the Rebellion: The Official Records of the Union and Confederate Armies*, 128 vols. (Washington D.C., 1890-1901), series I, volume 11, part 2, 424.

[10] The Battle of Beaver Dam Creek, also called the Battle of Mechanicsville, cost Robert E. Lee's army more than fifteen hundred casualties while the Federal defenders lost fewer than four hundred.

[11] Neither Colonel C. Feger Jackson, commander of the Ninth Pennsylvania Reserves, nor Colonel James T. Kirk, the Tenth's commander, mentioned this incident in their reports on the battle, which suggests that Company A's error, happily, caused no significant damage to the Ninth. *Official Records*, I, 11, pt. 2, p. 422-425.

Chapter 1 — Wounded

[12] Private Joseph Stewart, Company F, Tenth Pennsylvania Reserve Volunteer Corps (Thirty-ninth Pennsylvania Volunteer Infantry), was mustered in June 19, 1861, for three years or the duration of the war. Born in Glasgow, Scotland, Stewart was twenty-two years old in 1862, stood five feet, eight inches with light blue eyes, fair complexion and light brown hair. He was a miner before the war. He sustained at Gaines's Mill, according to a 1904 report of an examining surgeon, "GSW [gunshot wound] right side of face, ball entered right cheek 3/4 to right of the angle of the mouth, passed backwards and downward to exit below the angle of the lower jaw one inch below and posterior to lobe of the ear, fracturing both upper and lower jaws, also a scar one inch below angle of jaw where pieces of bones were removed, the scars not adherent, paralysis of muscles of right cheek, unable to close right eyelids producing great deformity of face on account of loss of substansive [sic] bone in lower and upper Jaw." The wound also cost Stewart the hearing in his right ear. The government discharged Stewart October 6, 1862, due to his wounds, and he returned to his home near Vale Summit, Maryland, a few miles from Roy's mother's home. Despite the pain, disability and disfigurement caused by his wounds, Stewart was able to persuade a courageous woman to marry him in December 1863 (see Roy's comments on the wedding in chapter 16). Andrew Roy was his best man. Joseph and Elizabeth Stewart produced eight children. She died in 1910, and he followed in 1917. Bates, *History of Pennsylvania Volunteers*, vol. 1, p. 835; Stewart Service Record and Pension File, National Archives. Bates erroneously states that Stewart was wounded in the Battle of Charles City Cross Roads (more commonly known as the Battle of Glendale), fought June 30, 1862, three days after the Battle of Gaines's Mill.

[13] It is not possible to identify the battery Roy saw in action, but circumstantial evidence suggests the cannons belonged to Captain William B. Weeden's Battery C, First Rhode Island Light Artillery. Of Weeden's six guns, two were commanded by Lieutenant W. W. Buckley. Confederate infantry overran Buckley's position and captured his two cannon. *Official Records*, I, 11, pt. 2, p. 282.

[14] Roy refers to both the regiment's surgeon and assistant surgeon. David McKinney was mustered in as assistant surgeon of the Tenth Pennsylvania Reserves June 29, 1861. He was promoted to surgeon of the 134th Pennsylvania Volunteer Infantry September 1, 1862. Benjamin Rohrer served the Tenth Reserves as surgeon for its

entire three-year enlistment, from June 1861 to June 1864. Bates, *History of Pennsylvania Volunteers*, vol. 1, p. 824.

[15] Roy refers to the troops of the Regular U.S. Army, as opposed to the volunteer troops, like himself, who had enlisted to help fight the war. The eleven regiments of Regulars at Gaines's Mill were grouped into one division under the command of Brigadier General George Sykes. Sykes's division played a major role in the battle by stemming the Confederate advance. Zouaves were volunteer troops that had adopted the flamboyant uniforms of the famed French troops. Roy probably refers to the men of the Fifth New York Infantry, "Duryea's Zouaves," who fought tenaciously at Gaines's Mill.

[16] General Thomas Meagher's Irish Brigade. Roy suggested here that because of the shouting "Stonewall Jackson thought our men were rallying, and General Whiting dispatched an aide to General Longstreet for reinforcements." Roy, of course, had no way of knowing what Jackson thought, so his speculation is based on post-war reading and is at best hearsay.

[17] Captain Milo Romulus Adams led Company F at Gaines's Mill [*see* note 20 below]. Company F's first lieutenant at Gaines's Mill was Ephriam P. Stewart, who had been mustered in as first sergeant June 29, 1861, and promoted to first lieutenant October 14, 1861. Stewart resigned August 20, 1862. Five men held the rank of sergeant in Company F at Gaines's Mill and it is impossible to determine which two visited the hospital that night. Rufus D. Cole was the company's top, or first, sergeant, and with both the captain and the first lieutenant visiting wounded men in the hospital, it is likely Cole, as ranking non-commissioned officer, would have remained with the rest of the company that night with Second Lieutenant Thomas L. Barragh. James M. Moorberger, James McKee, William Olcott and Harrison J. Chandler were the other sergeants, and any of them might have accompanied Adams and Stewart to the hospital. All four sergeants had been mustered in June 19, 1861. Moorberger and McKee were mustered out as sergeants June 11, 1864. Olcott reenlisted at the end of his three-year term of service and was transferred to the 191st Pennsylvania Volunteer Infantry June 1, 1864. Chandler was discharged for disability December 13, 1863. Bates, *History of Pennsylvania Volunteers*, vol. 1, p. 834.

[18] The captain's remarks probably represented an attempt to buoy the spirits of the desperately wounded Roy. Adams might or might not have believed his own words. Roy observed that "This report was spread through our lines and was generally believed. McClellan and Porter had discussed the feasibility of attacking Richmond the night after the battle of Mechanicsville, and the general was then impressed with his ability to break through Lee's weakened lines; but lost heart when the time came to attack." Roy is mistaken. McClellan had no intention of trying to break through to Richmond on the south side of the Chickahominy on June 27. The general had set no time for such an attack and therefore did not "lose heart" when the time came.

[19] Roy paraphrases from *The Tragedy of Macbeth* by William Shakespeare (1564-1616) English poet and playwright. "Had I as many sons as I have hairs, I would not wish them to a fairer death." act V, scene 8, lines 47-48. Lieutenant Evan Woodward of the Second Pennsylvania Reserves offers a glimpse of scenes on the

battlefield on the night of the twenty-seventh. "About eight o'clock, the battle ceased and we were moved some distance toward the rear, near a field hospital where the wounded were being continually brought in for surgical treatment, after which they were laid upon the grass, a blanket thrown over them, and a canteen of water put by their side, where some slept and others died. The poor fellows displayed most heroic fortitude, and though many of them were horribly mangled and suffering intense pain, only suppressed murmurs escaped their lips." Evan Woodward, *Our Campaigns* (Philadelphia, 1865), p. 96.

[20] Captain Milo R. Adams, Company F, Tenth Pennsylvania Reserve Volunteer Corps (Thirty-ninth Pennsylvania Volunteer Infantry), was a member of the class of 1853 at the U.S. Military Academy but did not graduate. Association of Graduates, *Register of Graduates and Former Cadets of the United States Military Academy* 1802-1990 (West Point, 1990), p. 277. He was a resident of Rochester, Pennsylvania, in 1861 and raised Company F in that vicinity. He was mustered in June 29, 1861, for three years or the war. The twenty-eight-year-old Adams stated that on June 30, 1862, in the Battle of Glendale, "A musket ball struck my left breast penetrating the lungs and passing out of my back near the spine." Comrades carried him from the field to a dressing station at Willis Church, where he was captured by Confederates the following day. With many others wounded in the fight, he remained on the battlefield under the care of Dr. James A. Skelton, who had charge of a temporary hospital at the Nelson House. Since the Confederates paroled Adams July 17, 1862, at Haxall's Landing on the north side of the James, rather than at City Point, on the south side, it seems likely that the Southerners did not transfer Adams to Richmond as they did Roy. Perhaps because of the severity of his wound, Adams may have remained at the Nelson House, which was but a few miles from Haxall's. Unlike Roy, Adams went directly to his home upon being exchanged. The government discharged him, on account of his wounds, December 25, 1862. Bates, *History of Pennsylvania Volunteers*, vol. 1, p. 834; Adams Service Record, National Archives.

[21] According to Lieutenant George W. McCracken, adjutant of the Tenth Reserves, the regiment held its ground at Gaines's Mill, "until late in the evening, when, with ammunition exhausted and ranks sadly thinned, the whole line was forced to give way. . . ." McCracken declared after the war that the regiment suffered more at Gaines's Mill than in any of the fourteen other battles in which it participated. McCracken recorded 140 casualties for June 27, 1862, — forty men killed and one hundred wounded. William Fox states that the Tenth sustained 134 casualties, twenty-three killed, eighty-six wounded, and twenty-five missing, and further states that nineteen of the 111 wounded or missing later died, bringing the mortality total to forty-two for the battle. Among the eleven and one-half regiments of McCall's at Gaines's Mill, only the Eleventh Pennsylvania Reserves suffered more casualties — seventy-one killed or mortally wounded, and nine of the regiment's ten companies were taken prisoner. Regimental adjutant McCracken reported that "the loss suffered by the Tenth Regiment at Gaines's Mill was numerically the greatest it ever sustained, although the percentage of loss out of the number engaged was much greater at Manassas, and also at Fredericksburg . . ." McCracken, "Address," *Pennsylvania at Gettysburg*, vol. 1, p. 265; Fox, *Regimental Losses*, pp. 259-260.

[22] Private Michael C. Lowry was mustered into Company A, Tenth Pennsylvania Reserve Volunteer Corps (Thirty-ninth Pennsylvania Volunteer Infantry) June 20, 1861, for three years or the duration of the war. He was a native of Somerset, Pennsylvania, and the son of Michael and Sarah Lowry. His father died in 1839, the same year the boy was born, and Sarah remarried two years later. Her second husband, Joseph Sahrie, died fifteen years later in 1856, so Michael was left to support his mother. After joining the army, he sent a portion of his pay home. At the age of twenty-three, he was wounded in the thigh at the Battle of Gaines's Mill and spent several months recuperating in prison and in Federal hospitals. He rejoined his regiment December 13, 1862, and was killed later that day in the Battle of Fredericksburg. Bates, *History of Pennsylvania Volunteers,* vol. 1, p. 836. Lowry Service Record and Pension File, National Archives. See Roy's relation of these events in chapter 16.

[23] This "band belt," which figures prominently later in Roy's story, apparently belonged to a member of the regimental band. Civil War regiments often marched, and sometimes fought, to musical accompaniment. Bandsmen usually served as stretcher bearers in battle. Many regimental commanders broke up their bands in 1862.

Chapter 2 — The Humanities of War

[24] Roy refers to Libby Prison, formerly a warehouse. See chapter 8.

[25] Unfortunately, it is impossible to positively identify the plantation house at which Roy and his comrades sojourned at Gaines's Mill. The evidence, as presented by Roy, suggests two possibilities, but neither place can reconcile itself completely with Roy's account. The home of Mr. Joseph A. Adams lay perhaps half a mile behind the Federal battle line on which Roy was wounded and was the house closest to the fighting, excepting the Watt House, which late in the battle became engulfed by the fighting, so could not be the structure Roy came to know. Roy was transported by ambulance to the regimental hospital, thence by stretcher to the "mansion." Given the short distance involved, and given that Mr. Adams, like the plantation owner in Roy's account, had evacuated his wife and children before the battle and came back to visit his property in the days following the fight, it would seem likely that Roy was laid down at the Adams farm. Furthermore, Assistant Surgeon W. E. Waters, U.S. Army, stated that "the principal hospital for the division [Morell's or Sykes's] was a large house about one-third of a mile in the rear of the line of battle." This description fits the Adams House. However, other evidence suggests Roy's place of rest was not the Adams place. The forty-five-year-old Adams did have a son of the age to enjoy a pony and did lose an enormous amount of property to the Federal occupiers of his farm, but in the lengthy, laboriously compiled claims filed against the government in the 1870s, in which he asked compensation of between eight thousand and fourteen thousand dollars and mentioned everything from hams to shoats to threshed wheat, Adams declared no pony. Furthermore, a house so close to the center of the Federal battle line in an engagement in which thirty-one hundred Federal soldiers were wounded would likely be a depository for scores, perhaps hundreds, of casualties. Assistant Surgeon H. S. Schell, Ninety-fourth New York Volunteers, reported that "nearly three hundred wounded men were accumulated" at the hospital depot he

established around the Adams House early in the battle. Roy does not leave the impression that his hospital was so crowded. Finally, the Adams house, though substantial, hardly fits the modern idea of a "mansion," though it is impossible to know what picture this word conjured up for Roy. He might have reposed on the property identified on post-war maps as the William Martin House, south of the Adams House and half a mile farther from the battle line. The house no longer stands and we know nothing of the Martins or whoever owned the property in 1862. See Adams's claims and census information about his property in files at Richmond National Battlefield Park and Schell's report in *The Medical and Surgical History of the Civil War*, 12 volumes (Washington, D.C.), vol. 2, pp. 76, 80.

[26] Roy refers again to the U.S. Army troops of George Sykes's division.

[27] Surgeons in the Civil War used chloroform on patients as a general anesthetic. Breathing chloroform vapor induces loss of consciousness. Roy's allusion to the British army at Flanders is not clear, but may emanate from the novel *Tristram Shandy* by Laurence Sterne (1713-1768). In book III, chapter 11 (written in 1761 and 1762), the character Uncle Toby says, "Our armies swore terribly in Flanders, but nothing compared to this." Flanders lies on the eastern shore of the North Sea at the border between Belgium and France. Uncle Toby was a veteran of war service under William of Orange in the War of the Grand Alliance (1688-1697) and was wounded at the 1695 Siege of Namur.

[28] Simplex cerrate was a simple ointment used for dressing wounds and composed of lard or oil mixed with wax or rosin.

[29] Charles Louis Napoleon Bonaparte (1808-1873), emperor of France and nephew of Napoleon Bonaparte, was known as both Louis Napoleon and Napoleon III. He agitated against the French monarchy, led or supported revolts, endeared himself to the peasantry, and became emperor in 1852.

Chapter 3 — A War of Words

[30] Here Roy indulged in a musing on Stonewall Jackson, "But notwithstanding his modest and unassuming bearing he was, I verily believe, the ablest general which the Civil War produced on either side. He was killed too early in the war to fill a large space in its history. Had his life been spared the war might have had a different ending. It was at Jackson's suggestion that Lee assumed the offensive in the campaign of the Seven Days' Fight, and so skillfully did Stonewall mask his movements in leaving the valley to reinforce Lee, that neither Shields nor Fremont, who were in his front to hold him there; nor the Secretary of War, nor McClellan, knew anything about his position until he suddenly appeared on McClellan's right flank and put the Union general on the defensive. "While he lived he was Lee's strong right arm. Lee never lost a battle when Jackson was with him; he never gained a victory after Jackson was killed. Cromwell and Jackson were men of the same stamp; both trusted in God, but kept their powder dry; both were alike invincible in war. Next to Cromwell, England never produced a general of equal ability to Jackson — not even the Iron Duke. But he was fighting against the civilization and enlightened public sentiment of the nineteenth century, and that God to whom he so often and so devoutly prayed to vouchsafe his blessings on the Confederate cause, could not smile with approval on the upbuilding of a

nation founded on a corner-stone of slavery." Roy is incorrect in attributing to Jackson the idea to attack McClellan's vulnerable right flank. General Robert E. Lee gave birth to the idea and discussed it with Confederate President Jefferson Davis in May 1862. Lee informed Jackson and other commanders of the plan June 23, 1862.

[31] Charles Sumner (1811-1874), U.S. Senator from Massachusetts; Horace Greeley (1811-1872), founder and editor of the New York *Tribune;* and William Lloyd Garrison (1805-1879), publisher of *The Liberator*, were all vocal advocates of the immediate abolition of slavery. Garrison's newspaper was perhaps the most important voice of Abolitionism before the Civil War. Sumner was a leader of the extreme wing of the Republican party known as the Radicals, and Greeley's influential *Tribune* consistently goaded the Lincoln administration toward more concrete and immediate action in freeing slaves and punishing the South.

[32] Philip Dormer Stanhope, Fourth Earl of Chesterfield (1694-1773), British diplomat, member of Parliament, and man of letters, wrote a series of letters to his illegitimate son, Philip Stanhope, which were published after his death as *Letters to his Son on the Fine Art of Becoming a Man of the World and a Gentleman*. This and other collections of letters by Chesterfield were widely read in the nineteenth century and established the author's renown as a model gentleman.

[33] Private Thomas Hawley, Company F, Tenth Pennsylvania Reserves, was mustered into the army June 19, 1861, at the age of twenty-two. He was killed in action one year and eleven days later at the Battle of Glendale. Private Hugh McMillan (or McMillen) was twenty-one years old when he was mustered in to Company F, Tenth Pennsylvania Reserves. He fell dead August 30, 1862, in the Battle of Second Manassas. Bates, *History of Pennsylvania Volunteers,* vol. 1, p. 835. Hawley and McMillan Service Records, National Archives.

[34] Troops on both sides of the Civil War wore woolen tunics — part of their undress uniform — that they referred to as blouses.

Chapter 4 — Fighting Maggots and Mosquitoes

[35] The poem that serves as the basis for "Annie Laurie" was written in Scottish dialect by William Douglas around 1800 and set to music by Lady John Douglas Scott (1810-1900). The song was published in 1838 and is said to have been as popular among British troops in the Crimean War as it was among Roy and his comrades. Denis Arnold, ed. *New Oxford Companion to Music*, 2 vols. (Oxford, 1983), vol. 1, p. 87. See Margaret Boni Bradford's *Fireside Book of Folk Songs* (New York, 1947).

[36] H. S. Schell, assistant surgeon in the Ninety-fourth New York Infantry, voluntarily became a prisoner of war when he stayed with the wounded on the battlefield of Gaines's Mill while the rest of the Federal army withdrew. He worked with one other surgeon at a house somewhere on the battlefield caring for 120 wounded men. In a report filed months later, he remarked upon the sufferings of the wounded. "The ration furnished for the patient by the Confederate authorities consisted of flour and bacon, with a small proportion of beans, salt beef, and salt. The quantity was exceedingly small, and many of the poor wretches forgot the pain of their injuries in the more terrible pangs of hunger. But while food was scarce, maggots were abundant, crowding and rolling in every wound, and

searching beneath the dressings to fasten upon every excoriation. Oil of turpentine and infusion of tobacco and of the flowers of the elderberry were tried, for the purpose of getting rid of this pest; but the most effectual means was found to be the dressing forceps; and to keep a wound clean, it required to be examined every two or three hours. A solution of camphor in oil, is an excellent remedy, if applied directly to the bodies of the intruders, the secretions of the wound having been previously removed by a piece of sponge. It seems to me that the maggot actually does damage in a wound; although not by attacking the living tissues, but only by the annoyance created by the continual sensation of crawling and irritation which it occasions, and of which the patient often complains bitterly. In certain states of the system, the nervous excitement or irritability thus engendered must react injuriously upon the parts." *Medical and Surgical History of the Civil War,* vol. 2, page 76.

[37] William T. Sherman (1820-1891), Union general, delivered his most famous utterance in the commencement address at the Michigan Military Academy June 19, 1879. "War is at best barbarism. . . .Its glory is all moonshine. It is only those who have neither fired a shot nor heard the shrieks and groans of the wounded who cry aloud for blood, more vengeance, more desolation. War is hell." See *National Tribune,* Washington, D.C., November 26, 1914.

Chapter 5 — Hard Times

[38] Jackson's troops crossed the Chickahominy River in pursuit of McClellan on the morning of June 30, 1862, using Grapevine Bridge.

[39] Roy quotes from *The Vicar of Wakefield* by the Irish poet and novelist Oliver Goldsmith (1728-1774). Goldsmith's lines from his 1766 novel recall those of poet Edward Young (1683-1765), who in *Night Thoughts,* finished in 1745, wrote "Man wants but little, nor that little long." (Canto IV, line 118).

[40] According to the log of the *U.S.S. Galena,* a gunboat anchored in the James River about fifteen miles from Gaines's Mill, rain fell in measurable amounts only twice between June 27 and July 13, 1862, the date Confederates moved Roy and his comrades to Richmond. Rain fell in torrents on the night of June 29 and into the pre-dawn hours of June 30, and a heavy rain began falling at sunrise on July 2 and continued through the day. The watch on the *Galena* recorded temperatures for thirteen of the sixteen days Roy spent exposed to the elements on the battlefield. The average of the recorded temperatures was just under 81 degrees. The low recorded temperature during that period was 60 degrees, on the afternoon of rainy July 2, and the high mercury reading was 102 degrees, at 11:00 A.M. on July 10. Log of the *U.S.S. Galena,* Record Group 24, National Archives, Washington, D.C.

[41] The text reads "If".

[42] Roy echoes Shakespeare's *The Tragedy of King Lear:*
> "Poor naked wretches, wheresoe'er you are,
> That bide the pelting of this pitiless storm,
> How shall your houseless heads and unfed sides,
> Your looped and windowed raggedness, defend you
> From seasons such as these?" act III, scene iv, lines 28-32.

[43] There is no evidence that Confederate President Jefferson Davis or anyone else in the Confederate government deliberately withheld food or medical supplies from Federal prisoners. It is probably fair to say that the delay in attending to the wants of prisoners and wounded men on the fields of the Seven Days Battles were due to the immense number of wounded and the chaos inherent to a week-long running battle. Taken together, the Seven Days Battles were by far the largest battles of the war up to that point, producing almost twenty thousand Confederate casualties and costing the Federals more than fifteen thousand men. The Confederacy, which retained control of the fields of battle, was understandably overwhelmed for a time by the task of providing for the thousands of helpless men left behind by the armies. Testimony from Federal surgeons who remained with the wounded and thus became prisoners of war indicates that Robert E. Lee and Stonewall Jackson cooperated fully with medical personnel caring for wounded Federals.

[44] Hardtack — also known as hard bread, army bread, pilot bread and army crackers — was a large, thick cracker that served as a staple of the diet of troops in both armies. Unsavory even when fresh, hardtack was often issued to the troops when stale or even moldy. The men sometimes fried it in grease or broke it up to add body, but not flavor, to soups and stews concocted around their campfires.

[45] The text omits the closing quotation mark.

[46] Private Robert A. Sayers, Company I, Eighth Pennsylvania Reserve Volunteer Corps (Thirty-seventh Pennsylvania Volunteer Infantry), was a twenty-year-old student from Waynesboro, Pennsylvania, when he enlisted in the army in November 1861. He stood 5'11-3/4" tall with a light complexion, brown hair and gray eyes. Sayers was wounded in the thigh at Gaines's Mill, June 27, 1862, and was apparently moved thence by comrades to the Federal hospital at Savage's Station, where the Federal army abandoned him and approximately twenty-five hundred other men too incapacitated to move. The Confederates made him a captive at Savage's Station June 30, 1862. The Southerners confined him at Richmond from July 13, 1862, until his parole on August 3 at City Point. Sayers recuperated at the U.S. Army General Hospital at Chester, Pennsylvania, in August, 1862. He returned to duty and, on May 15, 1864, was transferred to the 191st Pennsylvania Volunteer Infantry. Bates, *History of Pennsylvania Volunteers*, vol. 1, p. 781; Sayers Service Record, National Archives, Washington, D.C.

Chapter 6 — The Classics

[47] William Shakespeare (1564-1616), English poet and playwright; George Gordon, Lord Byron (1788-1824), English poet; Robert Burns (1759-1796), Scottish poet (*see* note 49 below). *Paradise Lost* (1667), the best-known work of English poet John Milton (1608-1674), is considered one of the masterworks of English literature.

[48] Roy quotes *Paradise Lost*, Book VI, lines 856ff, which read:

". . . and as a Herd
Of Goats or timorous flock together throng'd
Drove them before him Thunder-struck, pursu'd
With terrors and with furies to the bounds

And Crystal wall of Heav'n, which op'ning wide,
Roll'd inward, and a spacious Gap disclos'd
Into the wasteful Deep;"

Staunch Unionist Roy here indulged in a strained comparison between the rebellion of the Southern states and Satan's war on heaven: "Whoever has read Book VI of Paradise Lost must have been struck with the parallel between the Civil War in Heaven, and the Civil War in the United States. Both wars had their origin against constitutional authority. Satan and his followers rebelled, because, the Almighty had selected His Only Begotten Son to be the head of the government in Heaven; Jeff. Davis and his followers rebelled because the voice of the people, which is the voice of God, had selected Abraham Lincoln to be the head of the government in the United States. Satan's army was successful in the early part of the war; Jeff. Davis' army was successful in the early part of the war. Satan's Rebellion ended in sudden collapse; the Southern Rebellion ended in sudden collapse. Satan was imprisoned in Hell; Jeff Davis in Fortress Monroe. Neither of these great leaders ever asked for pardon."

[49] Robert Burns wrote verse in the dialect spoken by the common people of Scotland. He wrote of young love, of farming and hard labor, of drinking and revelry with friends, all themes close to the honest folk among whom he lived. Burns's tender sentimentality and unabashed love of the hardy land and people of his homeland made him immensely popular, and Roy, like a great many of his countrymen, idolized him. Burns is the national poet of Scotland. *Tam O'Shanter* (1790) is among his best-known works.

[50] Henry Wadsworth Longfellow (1807-1882) American poet, William Cullen Bryant (1794-1878), American poet, essayist and editor and John Greenleaf Whittier (1807-1892), American poet, were all exceptionally popular in their time.

Chapter 7 — A Change of Base

[51] "Change of Base" became something of a catch phrase in the Union Army of the Potomac after the Seven Days Battles. In the face of Lee's attacks on June 26 and 27, 1862, McClellan withdrew from his front lines outside of Richmond and spent a week in a fighting withdrawal to positions on the James River. During this movement, McClellan shifted his enormous base of supplies from White House Landing on the Pamunkey River to Harrison's Landing on the James. Though the transition looked to most observers like a retreat occasioned by vigorous Confederate attacks, McClellan fashioned the movement a "change of base." Thereafter, soldiers in both armies wryly used "change of base," as a euphemism for a retreat. Roy's use of the phrase here recalls its popularity but not its irony.

[52] Rachel, wife of Jacob, mother of Joseph and Benjamin and daughter of Laban, makes her appearance in the Book of Genesis, chapter 29. Roy refers to the incident in the Book of Jeremiah (31:15-17) in which the disconsolate Rachel weeps for her children who have been taken from her: "Thus saith the LORD; A voice was heard in Ramah, lamentation, *and* bitter weeping; Rachel weeping for her children refused to be comforted for her children, because they *were* not. Thus saith the LORD; Refrain thy voice from weeping, and thine eyes from tears: for thy work shall be rewarded, saith the LORD; and they shall come again from the

land of the enemy. And there is hope in thine end, saith the LORD, that thy children shall come again to their own border."

[53] The Richmond & York River Railroad was finished in 1857 to convey passengers and freight between Richmond and West Point, a port town at the head of the York River. During the Peninsula Campaign, the railroad served as the Federal army's main supply line. Savage's Station had been a major forward depot for supplies since late-May 1862, and had become a Federal hospital in the early days of June, following the Battle of Seven Pines fought on May 31 and June 1. When McClellan retreated south of the Chickahominy and on toward the James River, Confederate troops under Major General John Bankhead Magruder attacked the strong Federal rear guard at Savage's on the afternoon of June 29. The Federals repulsed these attacks, but retreated after dark. The last Federal troops at Savage's Station departed on the morning of June 30, leaving between two thousand and twenty-five hundred sick and wounded men behind in the hospital tents. Federal surgeons, most civilian doctors from the North who had come voluntarily to serve the army on the Peninsula, remained behind to care for the wounded.

[54] Roy's Service Record states that he was confined in Richmond on July 13, 1862. This might represent a clerical error or Roy might be in error in stating that he went to the city on July 15. The service records of Privates Campbell, Lowry and Sayers, all comrades mentioned by Roy, state they were confined at Richmond on July 13, 1862. Roy Service Record, National Archives, Washington, D.C.

[55] The swampy nature of the Chickahominy region hindered military operations until the armies artificially surfaced the soft roads with fallen trees — a process called corduroying. Under the direction of the Federal army engineers, Northern soldiers had in May and June corduroyed long stretches of roads on the Peninsula Corduroyed roads deteriorated rapidly under heavy traffic and required much maintenance. Even under the best of circumstances, the ride in a wagon passing over the fallen logs was not comfortable, as Roy attests.

[56] Belle Isle, an island in the James River at Richmond, served as a prisoner of war camp for enlisted soldiers. Like most Civil War prisons, it was overcrowded and unsanitary. In early 1864, the Confederacy moved most of the ten thousand captives at Belle Isle to a new prison at Andersonville, Georgia.

[57] Though probably impossible for Roy to admit in 1862 that his army had been beaten in the Seven Days, and apparently no easier for him to admit the possibility forty years later when he wrote his book, the portrait of the Seven Days offered by the Richmond papers, as Roy recounts it here, was far from "a monstrous caricature." Though the Federal soldiers fought well in the Seven Days and were successful in all their battles that week except at Gaines's Mill, the Richmond editors were justified in their summary of the week's result. McClellan's army had been driven back and did seek protection from U. S. Navy gunboats in the James River. While morale in the Federal army remained high through the Seven Days and for some time afterward, McClellan himself seemed to have lost the heart to fight after Lee's army defeated his troops at Gaines's Mill.

[58] Savage's Station lay about eight miles from the train station in Richmond along the Richmond & York River Railroad.

[59] This is a reference to the fervor of religious leaders, particularly in New England,

who preached the abolition of slavery as the will of God. Some Southerners considered Abolitionists the true instigators of the war.

[60] Dante Alighieri (1265-1321), Italian poet, wrote *Inferno* as part of *The Divine Comedy* (c. 1310-1320). The inscription at Dante's gates of Hell reads, in part: "All hope abandon, ye who enter here." Canto III, line 9.

Chapter 8 — New Quarters

[61] Roy's new quarters were in Libby Prison. In 1845, John Enders raised fourteen buildings as warehouses for tobacco and other products transported by ships in the James river and a nearby canal. One Luther Libby leased one of these warehouses and even after Confederate authorities took control of the three-story structure for use as a prison, the sign "L. Libby & Son, Ship Chandlers" remained on the facade, and Federal prisoners came to call the prison "Libby's." Libby Prison stood at what is today the corner of Cary and Twentieth Streets in Richmond. If the warehouse prison in which Roy spent his first night in Richmond was "on the same street," it may have been one of the buildings that came to be known as Castle Thunder or Castle Lightning. Both former warehouses housed civilian prisoners, spies, deserters and other "special" prisoners, so it would have been unusual for common military prisoners of war to have been detained there. Castle Thunder and Castle Lighting stood on what is now Cary Street about a block and a half from Libby. Once Roy reached Libby, he took up residence on the left side of the large room on the third floor. The red brick facades of Libby reached for more than three hundred feet along Cary Street on the north and Dock Street on the South. The prison consisted of three distinct but connected buildings, each with a separate entrance. That Roy's POW record states he was in Prison No. 2 suggests, perhaps, that he lived in the middle building. Directly across Dock Street lay the Kanawha Canal and the James River. Samuel T. Moore, Jr., *Moore's Complete Civil War Guide to Richmond* (Richmond, 1978), pp. 77-79.; Sandra V. Parker, *Richmond's Civil War Prisons* (Lynchburg, 1990), pp. 9-10.; Roy Service Record, National Archives, Washington, D.C.

[62] The chief surgeon at Libby in early 1862 was Dr. Edward Garrigues Higginbotham (1824-1901), a native Virginian who took his medical degree from the University of Pennsylvania in 1845. He served as surgeon for the elite militia unit the Richmond Virginia Grays and was appointed surgeon in the Confederate States Army. He founded the hospital at Libby where, according to one account, "his success in the treatment of typhoid fever and of the wounded was so remarkable that he was court martialed on suspicion of favoring the Union." He was cleared of charges and served subsequently in the field with the Third Corps, Army of Northern Virginia. *University of Pennsylvania Men in the Civil War: The Alumni Register* (Philadelphia, n.d.), p. 481.

[63] A member of the Thirteenth Pennsylvania Reserves, who, like Roy, had been taken prisoner in the Seven Days Battles and was confined in Libby concurrently with Roy, wrote: ". . .the accumulated filth of twenty months lay upon the floor or scampered up the walls of our gloomy prison; old tobacco quids, and other remnants of the first Bull Run victims still occupied, in undisturbed security, the various cracks and crevices. . . .When all had retired for the night, it was with

difficulty that one could walk from one end of the room to another, and without greatly incommoding the sleepers; and many were the anathemas, mental and verbal, showered upon the fellow who tried it. If our keepers were in good humor, our rations were served out to us twice a day. They consisted of a quarter of a small loaf of bread—invariably sour, and a very limited quantity of soup, in which the principal ingredient seemed to be flies. Not one in ten of the prisoners had a cup or dish of any description, and none were furnished us. Those who had money could send out and buy tin cups holding about a gill each, for which they were obliged to pay half a dollar. Those who had canteens tore off one side and used them for soup dishes; those who had neither cup, canteen nor money were compelled to borrow from their more fortunate companions, or let their soup go by default. Blocks of wood were scooped out to resemble bowls; strips of tin were eagerly seized and improvised into cups; pieces of wood split from the rafters were forced into service as spoons; in fact, a collection of the articles fashioned and used by the prisoners in Richmond would be a rare addition to any museum, illustrative both of the ingenuity of the makers as well as the barbarous usages that rendered them necessary." *The Trumansburg* (New York) *News*, January 30, 1863.

[64] Text reads "venders"

[65] Roy misquotes from *Paradise Lost*, Book I, lines 249ff, which read:
"Farewell happy fields
Where Joy for ever dwells: Hall horrors, hail
Infernal world, and thou profoundest Hell
Receive thy new Possessor; One who brings
A mind not to be chang'd by Place or Time;
The mind is its own place, and in itself
Can make a Heav'n of Hell, a Hell of Heav'n."

[66] "The worst is not, so long as we can say, 'This is the worst.'" *King Lear*, act IV, scene 1, line 27.

[67] Private Robert Campbell, Company F, Tenth Pennsylvania Reserves, was mustered in June 19 1861, at the age of nineteen. He was wounded in the thigh at Gaines's Mill, and remained on the battlefield until transferred to Richmond July 13, 1862. The Confederates confined him a prisoner of war in Libby Prison (third floor, left side of building), for about ten days until his exchange July 25, 1862, at City Point. Campbell returned to duty in March 1863, and served as an orderly for Major General Samuel Crawford from June 1863 to April 1864. He was mustered out with his company June 11, 1864. Bates, *History of Pennsylvania Volunteers*, vol. 1, p. 834; Campbell Service Record, National Archives.

[68] The Democratic Party tended to draw much of its strength from Southerners before and after the war.

Chapter 9 — Heartrending Scenes

[69] Though Libby later became known primarily as a prison for captured officers, during and after the Seven Days Battles, Confederate authorities consolidated wounded prisoners, all or mostly enlisted men, at Libby. Parker, *Richmond's Civil War Prisons*, p. 14.

[70] The most modern history of the prisons in Richmond contradicts Roy and reasserts that prisoners were sometimes shot for standing at windows. See Parker, *Richmond's Civil War Prisons*, p. 12.

[71] Roy quotes *Paradise Lost*, Book I, lines 47-48, which read:
"To bottomless perdition, there to dwell
In Adamantine Chains and penal Fire."
The passage refers to Satan's banishment from Heaven after his unsuccessful rebellion against God.

[72] Hemipterous: belonging or pertaining to the order Hemiptera comprising the heteropterous and homopterous insects. Roy uses the term to refer to body lice, which modern classification places in the order Anoplura. Roy's allusion to Burns could not be clarified.

[73] Civil War armies about to engage in combat formed into long lines of battle, perpendicular to the line of advance and parallel to the enemy line of battle. Before the battle was joined, both sides usually sent forward toward the enemy a group of riflemen known as "skirmishers," who advanced in a loose line abreast, ranged a few hundred yards ahead of the main line of battle and fought as individuals, taking advantage of trees, fences and other cover.

[74] One prisoner, a Lieutenant Colonel Williams, wrote a mock heroic tribute to the persistence of Libby's lice:
"But who, alas! so lazy, so busy, so nice,
Neglects to give an hour or two each day to lice,
Will be beset, at times, with troubles great and small,
And have dreadful scratching to get along at all.
If old poets wrote of battles 'twixt frogs and mice,
Why not I write of skirmishes 'twixt men and lice?
And while thus these verses rude we are inditing
Look 'round to see the different styles of fighting.
But I'll cease scratching lines and scratch 'Scotch fiddle' tunes
At something crawling in my shirt and pantaloons."
Parker, *Richmond's Civil War Prisons*, pp. 46-47.

[75] The free and unavoidable exchange of bacteria as the prisoners washed their bodies, wounds and bandages at this cistern behind Libby must have counteracted every practical benefit of "cleaning" the wounds.

[76] Brigadier General John Henry Winder, a Marylander, served as provost marshal in Richmond during Roy's stay there and as such had authority over all of the city's prisons. Lieutenant Thomas Pratt Turner, a native of White Post, Clarke County, Virginia, commanded Libby Prison in July 1862. He was but twenty-one years old when Confederate authorities appointed him to command at the prison. Richard R. Turner, no relation, served as second-in-command at the prison. He had been an overseer on a plantation near Richmond before the war. Parker, *Richmond's Civil War Prisons*, p. 11.

Chapter 10 — Poetry in Prison — Daydreams

[77] *Childe Harold's Pilgrimage* (1812-1818), a poetical travelogue of journeys through Europe, remains one of Byron's best-known works. Roy quotes stanza 45 of

Canto III, in which Childe Harold, having visited the battlefield at Waterloo, reflects on Napoleon. If this is the last of the eleven stanzas Roy and Lowry committed to memory, stanza 35 was the first.

[78] Roy refers to the segment in Canto III (published in 1816) beginning at stanza 21, line 181, which, alas, schoolboys no longer know by heart.

[79] Sir William Wallace (1272?-1305), Scottish general and patriot, remains one of Scotland's great heroes. Robert de Bruce VIII (1274-1329) king of Scotland (1306-1329).

[80] Roy's statement that the South was fighting "for slavery" does not imply that he was fighting primarily against slavery. He is clear that he was fighting to preserve the Union and in this he was typical of most Federal soldiers. Slavery was of secondary importance to him as a reason for going to war, though he apparently thought it was of primary importance to Southerners wishing to dissolve the Union. This, of course, was not universally or even largely true of Southerners, so Roy's generalization seems to be invalid.

[81] It is not clear whence Roy draws this quote, which seems an amalgamation. "Might makes right, and justice there is none." appeared in "Millennium" by the German poet Walther von der Vogelweide (c. 1170- c. 1230). "God is always for the big battalions" is attributed to a letter dated 1770 by Voltaire (pseudonym for Francois-Marie Arouet (1694-1778)) French essayist and satirist. Voltaire echoes statements by Frederick the Great (1712-1786), soldier and king of Prussia (1740-1786) in 1760 and Roger de Bussy-Rabutin (1618-1693), French count, ("God is usually on the side of the big squadrons and against the small ones." (1677)). See John Bartlett *Familiar Quotations*, fifteenth edition, edited by Emily Morison Beck (New York, 1980).

[82] Roy once again quotes Byron and *Childe Harold's Pilgrimage*, this time Canto III, stanza 21, line 186.

Chapter 11 — Discussing the Campaign

[83] Roy errs on one of the three counts. Assuming Roy was writing in 1904, the year the first edition of his book was published, the senior general in the U. S. Army was Major General Adna Romanza Chaffee, who served as senior general from 1904 to 1906 and had begun his military career in 1861 as a private in Company K, Sixth U.S. Cavalry. Preceding Chaffee as senior general was Major General Samuel Baldwin Marks Young, who, in 1861, was a private in Company K of the Twelfth Pennsylvania Volunteer Infantry. Young was commanding general for only a short time in 1903 and 1904. Nelson Appleton Miles was the senior general from 1895 to 1900 as a major general and from 1900 to 1903 as a lieutenant general. Miles was not a private in the Civil War. He began the war in 1861 as first lieutenant in the Twenty-second Massachusetts Volunteer Infantry. If Roy added this comment to his second edition, published in 1909, he might have been referring to Major General John Coalter Bates, who attained top rank in the Army in 1906. Bates began the Civil War as a first lieutenant in the Eleventh U.S. Infantry. Despite his error, Roy's point is nonetheless worthy of consideration: Perhaps only in America could private soldiers rise to command the nation's armies. Francis B. Heitman, *Historical Register and Dictionary of the United States*

Army 1789-1903, 2 vols. (Washington, 1903), vol. 1, pp. 17, 19-20, 199, 292, 708-709, 1067.

[84] Roy presents his opening two paragraphs with all the earnest sincerity and authority of a volunteer private in the Union army.

[85] The Battle of Austerlitz, December 2, 1805, at which Napoleon defeated the combined forces of Austria and Russia, is considered by some to have been the Corsican's tactical masterpiece. Napoleon deployed his army so as to entice the Allies to attack his weak and ill-positioned right. The Austro-Russians eagerly seized at the French bait, stripping their center of troops to launch attacks on the flank. Napoleon swiftly counterattacked with reserves in the enemy's weakened center. Victory came quickly as the Allies collapsed. Roy refers to McClellan's position through the first three weeks of June when the army was divided by the swampy Chickahominy River.

[86] Ulysses S. Grant (1822-1885), Union general and eighteenth president of the United States, and William T. Sherman (1820-1891) and Philip H. Sheridan (1831-1888), both Union generals, were all very aggressive in command of troops, Sheridan was extremely so. Roy's comments on McClellan's character are interesting because they illustrate that even at the time of Roy's writing critics ascribed the failure of the campaign to McClellan's character, not his plans. Though McClellan's post-war writings and the eloquent arguments of his supporters — both contemporaries and historians — argue that his strategy was undermined by interference from the Lincoln administration, most historians accept the argument put forth by Roy and others.

[87] Exasperated by the apparent idleness of Federal armies, Lincoln issued Special War Order No. 1 on January 31, 1862, directing that all the armies were to move on the enemy by February 22. McClellan protested the order and argued for more time. Lincoln's order might well have been just a ploy to force the hand of the secretive McClellan, who had not shared any of his plans for the spring campaigns. On February 3, the general did divulge his intentions for what became the Peninsula Campaign, and Lincoln did not enforce the requirement to move by February 22. Grant's February 1862 operations in Tennessee were highly successful and resulted in the capture of many thousands of Confederates (estimates of how many vary widely) at Forts Henry and Donelson. Fort Henry on the Tennessee River capitulated February 6, and Donelson on the Cumberland River surrendered on the 16th, well before the deadline of the 22nd imposed by Lincoln.

[88] George Gordon Meade (1815-1872) Union general, commanded the Army of the Potomac from June 1863 until the end of the war.

[89] This incident probably accurately illustrates the growing rift in the army between those soldiers who remained intensely loyal to McClellan and those who decided he was no longer worthy of their devotion.

[90] Roy refers to Napoleon's Italian Campaign (March 1796-April 1797).

[91] Roy seems to have omitted the name of the "detached" column. Context suggests he means to refer to Jackson, but, in truth, Lee did not "detach" Jackson, who had not yet joined Lee's army and was moving independently of Lee from the

Shenandoah Valley. It might accurately be said that Lee "dispatched" Jackson to fall on Porter's flank.

[92] "We had on hand but a limited amount of rations, and if we had advanced directly on Richmond it would have required considerable time to carry the strong works around that place, during which our men would have been destitute of food; and even if Richmond had fallen before our arms the enemy could still have occupied our supply communications between that place and the gunboats, and turned the disaster into victory." George B. McClellan, *McClellan's Own Story* (New York, 1887), p. 423.

[93] Roy slightly misrepresents McClellan's statement of killed and missing in both armies. McClellan gave the number of Confederate killed and missing as 2,823 and 3,223 respectively and the number of Union killed and missing as 1,745 and 6,043 respectively. That Roy's figures are off by one digit in each case suggests he or his publisher made errors in transcription. See *McClellan's Own Story* (New York, 1887), p. 440. The best sources readily available indicate the Army of Northern Virginia lost 19,557 men in the Seven Days and the Army of the Potomac lost 15,848. For the Confederate figures, see Jubal Early, "Strength of General Lee's Army in the Seven Days Battles Around Richmond," *Southern Historical Society Papers*, vol. 1, p. 421. See also *Official Records*, I, 11, pt. 2, pp. 973-984, and William Allan, *The Army of Northern Virginia in 1862* (Cambridge, Mass., 1892), p. 143ff. for a discussion of casualty figures. Allan counts 19,711. Contrast these reports with Dr. L. Guild in *Official Records* I, 11, pt. 2, pp. 502-510. For Federal losses, see McClellan's "Return of Casualties" in *Official Records* I, 11, pt. 2, pp. 24-37.

[94] The relative size of the armies in the Seven Days Battles continues to be a matter of dispute. Confederate records are imprecise, but on June 20, 1862, less than a week before he launched his attack at Beaver Dam Creek, Lee could count about 68,000 in his army. Another 16,000 to 18,500 or so under Jackson were enroute to join Lee. Then the two forces came together at Gaines's Mill on June 27, Lee had at his disposal between 80,000 and 85,000 men. On June 20, McClellan reported his army had a paper strength of 156,838 men, but that, due to sickness, desertions and special assignments, only 115,102 men were present for duty with their commands and ready to fight. For Confederate strengths, see G. F. R. Henderson, *Stonewall Jackson and the American Civil War* (New York, 1898, 1943, 1988), p. 345. In discussing Lee's strength in the Seven Days, Jubal Early proposes the figure 76,054 (including Jackson). He asserts Lee's army totaled no more that 80,000. Early, "Strength of General Lee's Army in the Seven Days Battles Around Richmond," pp. 421-422; Walter Taylor counted, 80,762 (Taylor, *Four Years with General Lee*, p. 53). Allan indicates Lee would have had about 80,000 after Jackson joined him. Allan, *The Army of Northern Virginia in 1862*, pp. 69. For McClellan's strength, see *Official Records* I, 11, pt. 3, p. 238.

Chapter 12 — Paroled

[95] Roy seems to be referring to the prison's medical director, Dr. E.G. Higginbotham.

[96] Roy celebrated his twenty-eighth birthday in Libby Prison on July 19, 1862. He was paroled six days later on July 25. Roy Service Record, National Archives, Washington, DC.

[97] "Black Hole" is slang for a military prison cell. The jail cell at Fort William, Calcutta, India, earned special notoriety among soldiers in the British army.

[98] City Point, Virginia, lies on the James River at the terminus of the Petersburg & City Point Railroad. Accessible by train and boat, it became a convenient place for the two armies to physically exchange paroled prisoners.

[99] In an aside, Roy explained that "Petersburg, two years later, became the theater of the operations of Grant's and Lee's armies. Its fall, after a prolonged and gallant defense, was followed by the capture of Richmond, the surrender of Lee's army and the total collapse of the Confederacy."

[100] Stentor was a Greek herald in the Trojan War renowned for his booming voice. Roy refers to Doxology (written in 1709) by Thomas Ken (1637-1711), bishop of Bath and Wells (1685-1691).
   "Praise God, from whom all blessings flow!
   Praise Him, all creatures here below!
   Praise Him above, ye heavenly host!
   Praise Father, Son, and Holy Ghost!"

[101] The steamer *Commodore* had served as McClellan's headquarters in mid-March 1862 when it had borne him to the Peninsula from Alexandria, Virginia.

[102] The *U.S.S. Monitor*, one of the more famous ships in naval history, was among the North's first ironclad warship. On March 9, 1862, it engaged the Confederate ironclad *C.S.S. Virginia* (nee *U.S.S. Merrimack*) in the famous first "duel between ironclads" in Hampton Roads, Virginia.

[103] Harrison's Landing was the ancestral seat of the Harrison family, of which Presidents Benjamin Harrison and William Henry Harrison were members. McClellan took his army there on July 2, 1862, in the hope that it could repose in safety protected by the U.S. Navy's gunboats in the James. Elements of the Federal army remained at Harrison's Landing until August 22, 1862.

[104] Many of the female nurses that served on the Peninsula were volunteers with the U.S. Sanitary Commission, a private benevolent organization that existed solely to bring comfort to and promote health among the soldiers of the Federal armies. During the war, the Sanitary Commission was a favored charity among the wealthy of the Northeast.

Chapter 13 — A Visit From the General

[105] McClellan penned these words to his wife Ellen on the night of July 26. On July 27, McClellan wrote to his wife "I can't tell you how glad I am that I went to see all those poor wounded men yesterday. Another batch will come tonight, & I will if possible go to see all of them tomorrow morning. I regard it as a duty I owe the poor fellows — rather a hard one to perform, but still one that cannot be neglected." McClellan visited the second load of wounded prisoners on the morning of July 28, taking with him, ". . . an armful of papers to give the poor fellows . . ." In his nightly letter of the 28th, the general told his wife, "Am very tired, for I saw and talked to every one of the wounded men to-day, being occupied all day at it." Roy states he was among the returned prisoners who met the general on the 26th, specifying that the meeting was on the day after he had left Richmond. This chronology is borne out by Roy's Service Record, which

states he was paroled on July 25. *McClellan's Own Story* (New York, 1887), p. 455-456.

[106] In the public mind, Oriental tales were characteristically full of magic and mystery. They were fantasies.

[107] Roy's phrasing is a trifle awkward. He refers to McClellan's willingness to shake the hand of every soldier returned from Confederate captivity.

[108] Henry Wager Halleck (1815-1872), Union general, served as general-in-chief of the Federal armies beginning in July of 1862 with headquarters in Washington. Though a sound administrator, he lacked the ability or will to exercise command in the field. John Pope (1822-1892), Union general, commanded a Federal army in Virginia in July 1862. McClellan deplored the division of Northern forces in the state and argued that Pope's men should be put under his command. The Lincoln administration demurred, and McClellan seems not to have energetically supported Pope's operations thereafter. Robert E. Lee outmaneuvered Pope in August 1862 and thrashed the Northerner's army at the Battle of Second Manassas August 29 and 30. Many observers thought McClellan deliberately withheld his assistance from Pope so his rival would be beaten and disgraced. See John J. Hennessy, *Return to Bull Run* (New York, 1992), pp. 49-50, 90-91, 128-129, 468-469.

[109] On August 3, 1862, Halleck ordered McClellan to begin withdrawing his army from the Peninsula. McClellan responded on August 4: "Your telegram of last evening is received. I must confess that it has caused me the greatest pain I ever experienced, for I am convinced that the order to withdraw this Army to Acquia Creek will prove disastrous in the extreme to our cause — I fear it will be a fatal blow." McClellan did not immediately act to implement the order and as late as August 10 was still talking privately of a "move forward in the direction of Richmond. . . ." The *Civil War Papers of George B. McClellan*, Stephen W. Sears, ed. (New York, 1989), pp. 383, 389; Hennessy, *Return to Bull Run*, pp. 10, 90-91, 128-129, 468-469.

Chapter 14 — Fort Monroe

[110] Roy refers again to English novelist, poet and playwright Oliver Goldsmith (1728-1774), but his allusion to "Goldsmith's sailor" could not be clarified.

[111] Roy and Lowry were admitted to the Chesapeake General Hospital at Fort Monroe July 27, 1862. Lowry was sent to the General Hospital at Annapolis on August 6, 1862. Roy Service Record and Lowry Service Record, National Archives, Washington, D.C.

[112] Roy attributes this witticism to Lee, who almost certainly never said it. Writers have attributed this much repeated statement to so many others that the true author of the remark is difficult to determine.

[113] Roy refers to Heaven and Hell.

[114] Roy was transferred to the General Hospital at Annapolis on August 24, 1862. Camp Parole lay about two miles west of Annapolis and was established in 1862 as a holding facility of Federal soldiers, like Roy, who had been prisoners of war. After parole, these soldiers could not fight until they were legally exchanged by the government. Union and Confederate authorities paroled prisoners to relieve

themselves of the burden of caring for them but would exact a promise from these prisoners that they would not fight again until both governments agreed that the soldier could do so. The authorities would periodically exchange lists of names of paroled prisoners who could then return to their regiments and resume fighting. The process often took several months. Camp Parole was temporary home to about seventy thousand soldiers during the war, but never more than about eight thousand at a time. The camps hospital included five buildings. Roy Service Record, National Archives, Washington, D.C.; Robert B. Roberts, *Encyclopedia of Historic Forts* (New York, 1988), pp. 387-388.

[115] James Norvall (or Norval) was enrolled as surgeon of the Seventy-ninth New York Volunteers, the Highlanders, June 1, 1861, but authorities never commissioned him. He served with the regiment in Virginia until the Confederates captured him at the Battle of Bull Run, July 21, 1861. His captors issued him a conditional parole August 2, 1861, so he could attend the wounded at Manassas, Virginia. The Confederates detained him briefly in Richmond in August, but paroled him August 11 and sent him to Federal-held Fort Monroe via Norfolk. His superiors directed him to take charge of the hospital at Camp Parole. Norvall, thirty-seven years old, was in command of the Camp Parole hospital in the fall of 1862, during which time Roy came for treatment. Norvall Service Record, National Archives; Frederick Phisterer, *New York in the War of the Rebellion*, 6 vols. (Albany, 1912), vol. 4, p. 2843; William Todd, *The Seventy-Ninth Highlanders New York Infantry in the War of the Rebellion 1861-1865* (Albany, 1886), p. 50.

[116] The Seventy-ninth New York Highlanders was a regiment in the New York State National Guard before the war and volunteered for Federal service in 1861. The men of the ranks were mostly Scots or descended from Scots. The regiment's dress uniforms included kilts for the officers and plaid trousers for the men. James Cameron, the regiment's first colonel during the war and brother of Simon Cameron, Lincoln's first secretary of war, was killed in action on Henry House Hill at the battle of Bull Run., July 21, 1861.

[117] Roy is mistaken in placing this event in South Carolina. The incident he refers to occurred during the defense of Fort Sanders near Knoxville, Tennessee, in November and December 1863. Todd, *The Seventy-Ninth Highlanders*, pp. 367-368, 386, 389. Robert de Bruce decisively defeated Edward II, king of England, at the Battle of Bannockburn in 1314. Though the English greatly outnumbered the Scots, Bruce made excellent use of the terrain and forced Edward's men to attack across marshy ground on a narrow front. The victory at Bannockburn permitted Scotland to establish its independence.

Chapter 15 — The Naval Academy

[118] The Naval Academy was founded in 1845 in Annapolis, Maryland on the Severn River as a naval school with a five-year program. The school was reorganized in 1850-1851 as the U.S. Naval Academy with a four-year program. At the outbreak of the Civil War in 1861, the Navy Department moved the school to temporary quarters in Newport, Rhode Island. The government used the vacant buildings at the Annapolis campus as a hospital. The Academy returned to Annapolis in 1865.

[119] Roy refers to bits of dead bone. Nekrosis is Greek meaning "deadness."

[120] During the Civil War, physicians more often used the abbreviation "GSW" for gunshot wound when completing a patient's record.

[121] In "charging bayonets," a soldier stood with one foot forward, as if striding, with both hands holding his weapon before his body, which was slightly bent at the waist with weight on the forward leg.

[122] Captain Milo Adams was wounded at the Battle of Glendale, June 30, 1862. *See* note 20, chapter 1

[123] Augustus Roy was born in Montreal, Canada, April 2, 1841. When he enlisted May 31, 1861 in Chicopee, Massachusetts, he was single and gave his occupation as upholsterer. He was mustered into Company F, Tenth Massachusetts Volunteer Infantry June 21, 1861. According to one regimental historian, Roy was "frightfully wounded in back of shoulder by a shell while lying in rifle-pits at Fair Oaks, Va., May 31, 1862; was sent next day to White House Landing [the Federal supply and hospital depot on the Pamunkey River twenty-three miles from Richmond] and from thence to Annapolis, Md., where he was in hospital more than eight months. . . ." Joseph Keith Newell, ed., *"Ours": Annals of Tenth Regiment Massachusetts Volunteers in the Rebellion* (Springfield, Mass., 1875), p. 509. The army discharged Roy March 4, 1863, at Boston on account of his wounds. Roy later served as a sergeant in Company A, Fifth Massachusetts Volunteer Militia, which was recruited to serve only a hundred days. He was mustered out of that organization November 16, 1864. After the war, Roy worked as a carriage painter in Springfield, Massachusetts, and, according to historian Newell in 1875, "still suffers from the effects of the wound." Roy died January 29, 1908. See Massachusetts Adjutant General, *Massachusetts Soldiers, Sailors and Marines in the Civil War*, 9 vols. (Norwood, Mass., 1931), vol. 1, pp. 713, 337, and Alfred S. Roe, *The Tenth Regiment Massachusetts Volunteer Infantry 1861-1864* (Springfield, 1909), p. 441.

[124] "I am happy to bear witness to the high character sustained, in this community, by all the members of the Roy family and I endorse a request from them more readily than I would from any others in this vicinity. Andrew Roy has received a good common education — he writes a good hand — and might become very useful in the Hospital Dept. after his wound is healed." M. M. Townsend [P.S.] By acceding to Roy's request — which I respectfully endorse — you may render him sooner fit for service — you will certainly confer great happiness upon his Mother — and you will much oblige Your Obt. Sert. M. M. Townsend, Act. Asst. Surgeon." Roy Service Record and Pension File, National Archives, Washington, D.C.

[125] Samuel Johnson, Ll.D. (1709-1784) English poet, essayist and critic, was born in Lichfield, Staffordshire, by the Trent River. Litchfield, Connecticut lies about twenty-five miles west of Hartford.

[126] Augustus Williamson Bradford (1806-1881) served as governor of Maryland from 1862 to 1866. An attorney before the war, Bradford had little experience in politics but was a staunch Unionist and so as candidate for governor in 1861 had the support of an anxious Lincoln administration. Though Bradford won office by a majority of thirty-one thousand votes, it seems likely that this imbalance was partly due to the administration's arrest of all members of the Maryland legislature

who were not strong Unionists. Though Bradford benefited from such heavy-handed coercion, he disliked it and opposed the Lincoln administration's efforts to influence subsequent elections in Maryland. When Confederates under General Jubal A. Early invaded Maryland in July 1864, a squad of soldiers traveled to Bradford's home about four miles from Baltimore and burned it to the ground, including all his possessions and his library. Ironically, Bradford's eldest son, William, served as a staff officer in the Confederate army. Federal troops apprehended him attempting to enter Washington in a wagon. When Governor Bradford heard the news, he paced silently for a few moments, then declared, "I have made up my mind; if William has come within our lines as a spy he must take the consequences. My duty to my official position will not permit me to take any action." Young William was spared when he successfully argued that he was not a spy but merely very ill and had been attempting to reach his father's home. Bradford was a sincere and forthright man, a devoted father (he had twelve children) and seems to have conducted his official business not as a politician but in the best tradition of a citizen serving his fellow citizens. *Dictionary of American Biography*, Allen Johnson and Dumas Malone, eds., 20 vols. (New York, 1943), vol. 2, pp. 553-555.

[127] The last battle that the Tenth Reserves participated in was at Bethesda Church, May 31, 1864. William Fox states the regiment lost only one man killed or mortally wounded in the engagement. Fox, *Regimental Losses*, p. 259.

[128] The Federal army fought the Battle of Fredericksburg on the south bank of the Rappahannock River, which it crossed on temporary, floating bridges constructed of planks laid over boat-like supports called pontoons. While we have no evidence of Lowry's gifts for command, his kindness and intelligence obviously made a strong impression on Roy.

Chapter 16 — Clarysville

[129] The government transferred Roy from the hospital at Annapolis to the General hospital at Clarysville December 29, 1862. Roy Service Record and Pension File, National Archives, Washington, D.C.

[130] Second Maryland Regiment Potomac Home Brigade was organized in Cumberland, Maryland, August 27, 1861, through October 31, 1861, for three years' service. Most of the men of the regiment were, like Roy, residents of Allegany County. The U. S. war department used these local troops to patrol the Maryland-Virginia border and guard the Baltimore and Ohio Railroad, the Chesapeake and Ohio Canal, and telegraph lines. Andrew Spier was mustered into Company A of the Second Maryland Regiment Potomac Home Brigade as second lieutenant August 1, 1861, and was promoted to first lieutenant January 28, 1862. He was mustered out September 28, 1864. L. Allison Wilmer, J. H, Jarrett, George W. F. Vernon, *History and Roster of Maryland Volunteers, War of the 1861-1865*, 2 vols. (Baltimore, 1898), vol. 1, p. 541, 544. Roy added: "The company which Lieutenant Spiers belonged to was raised in the Frostburg mining region, and was composed of miners, with all of whom I was personally acquainted. They were all stalwart Republicans, when it took nerve to be a Republican in a slave state. A number of these same men raised the first Republican campaign pole ever raised south of Mason and Dixon's line, and defended it with arms in their hands. The flag flew

to the breeze until it was blown to shreds and patches, was then cut down, the pole sawed into blocks about two inches square and an inch thick, and distributed all over the United States. In the year 1881 I put a piece in the show case of the relic room in the State House in Columbus [Ohio]." Wilmer, Jarrett and Vernon spell Spier's name without the "s" that Roy adds.

[131] Sir Archibald Alison (1792-1867) Scottish historian, lived in Roy's native Lanarkshire and published his *History of Europe* in 1833. He published new volumes and editions until his death. Roy perhaps did not know that Alison was an ardent supporter of the Confederacy. *British Authors of the Nineteenth Century*, edited by Stanley J. Kunitz (New York, 1936), p. 9. George Bancroft (1800-1891) American historian and diplomat, published his *History of the United States* in ten volumes between 1834 and 1874. *Dictionary of American Biography*, vol. 1, pp. 564-570.

[132] Surgeon J. B. Lewis had charge of the General Hospital at Cumberland, Maryland, in 1863.

[133] Dr. M. M. Townsend served as the assistant surgeon at the Clarysville general hospital in 1863.

[134] Castile soap is any hard soap made from fats and oils, especially a mild soap made from olive oil and sodium bicarbonate.

[135] Roy here wrote "Stuart."

[136] Roy breaks his chronological sequence here and jumps ahead nearly a full year to December 1863. Stewart was married December 18, 1863 in Vale Summit, Maryland. See note 1, Chapter 1. Stewart Pension File, National Archives, Washington, D.C.

[137] The object of Roy's attentions was Janet Watson, a native of Scotland. In a deposition dated October 1914, Janet stated she was sixty-eight years old, making her seventeen or eighteen years old at the Stewart wedding in December 1863, considerably younger than the twenty-nine-year-old Roy. Roy's account of his assault on the heart of "the high-spirited girl," echoes Othello's relation of his pursuit of the fair Desdemona in Shakespeare's *The Tragedy of Othello, the Moor of Venice* (c. 1600-1609). Othello won the favor of Brabantio, Desdemona's father, by reciting his adventures in battle:

> I ran it through, even from my boyish days
> To th' very moment that he bade me tell it. (act I, scene iii, lines 131-132)

Desdemona, much like Roy's saucy Janet, found her heart ensnared by the brave storyteller, and, as Othello relates:

> And bade me, if I had a friend that loved her,
> I should but teach him how to tell my story,
> And that would woo her. Upon this hint I spake.
> She loved me for the dangers I had passed,
> And I loved her that she did pity them. (act I, scene iii, lines 163-167)

Roy's closing remark recalls Othello's "She gave me for my pains a world of kisses" (act I, scene iii, line 158). See Roy's pension file, National Archives, Washington, D.C.

[138] After the war, Roy deposed he and Janet were married by the Rev. William Ellis on July 19, 1864, a Tuesday and his thirtieth birthday, at Eckhart Mines, Maryland. His obituary confirms this. Mrs. Roy, however, stated the wedding had been on July 12, 1864 (also a Tuesday), at Cumberland. Furthermore, Roy enlisted May 15, 1861, and was mustered in July 19, 1861 (his twenty-seventh birthday), not July 21, 1862, as he states here. Roy Service Record and Pension File, National Archives, Washington, D.C.; Roy Obituary, *The Wellston* (Ohio) *Sentinel*, October 21, 1914, p. 1.

[139] With this sentence, Roy returns to relating events of 1862.

[140] The text reads: "a pay from Uncle Sam."

[141] Some firearms of the Civil War era required small, thimble-like percussion caps containing chemical deposits. The shooter placed a cap on a nipple near the breech of the weapon and pulled the trigger. The hammer struck the cap, thereby creating a spark that ignited the powder charge and fired the bullet. The guns would not fire without the caps.

[142] Northern Democrats who favored a negotiated peace rather than a continuation of the war to preserve the Union were viewed as traitorous by many pro-Union Northerners and were referred to as "Copperheads," after the venomous snake of North America.

Chapter 17 — Surgical Operations

[143] Dr. James M. Porter was born at "Rose Meadows," the family farm near Frostburg, April 14, 1817, the seventh of eight children. In 1838, he began the study of medicine as apprentice to Drs. Samuel P. Smith and T. A. Healey, at Cumberland, Maryland. He attended medical lectures in Maryland and New York and received his medical diploma in 1842. In 1843, he moved to Frostburg and began his practice among the mining families there. According to one local historian, "His life has been spent almost entirely in the relief of suffering, and his good offices have been extended to the poor with no stinted hand." Dr. Porter was still alive as of 1882. J. Thomas Scharf, *History of Western Maryland*, 2 vols. (Philadelphia, 1882), vol. 2, pp. 1477-1478.

[144] Roy's refers to *Beside the Bonnie Briar Bush*, published in 1894, by Ian Maclaren, pseudonym of the Rev. John Watson (1850-1897), Scottish clergyman and author.

[145] Dr. Nathan Ryno Smith (May 21, 1897-July 3,1877) held the chair of surgery at the University of Maryland Medical School and was one of the eminent surgeons of his time. The son of a surgeon, Smith was a native of Cornish, New Hampshire, the same town that produced Abraham Lincoln's Secretary of the Treasury, Salmon P. Chase. After taking bachelor and medical degrees from Yale, Smith had a leading part in founding the medical school at the University of Vermont and had studied under Dr. George McClellan of Philadelphia, father of General George B. McClellan. Smith collaborated with Dr. McClellan in 1826 in establishing Jefferson Medical College in Philadelphia, which was to become one of the leading centers of medical education in the nineteenth century. Smith took the chair of anatomy at the University of Maryland Medical School in 1827 and transferred to surgery two years later, a position he would hold for nearly fifty

years. He wrote and lectured widely, edited several professional medical journals and gained a national reputation as a surgeon. He maintained friendships with both Henry Clay and Daniel Webster. One biographer described him thus: "Tall and impressive in appearance, Smith was called by his students 'The Emperor.' ... His imperial appearance was tempered, however, by a courtesy and charm of manner which endeared him to friends and patients." *Dictionary of American Biography*, vol. 9, pp. 327-329. See also Martin Kaufman, Stuart Galishoff, Todd L. Savitt, eds., *Dictionary of American Medical Biography*, 2 vols. (Westport, Conn., 1984), vol. 2, pp. 471-472, 696-697, and *Who Was Who in America, Historical Volume*, 1607-1896, (Chicago, 1967), p. 563.

[146] Colonel G. Ellis Porter, M.D., was born near Frostburg, Maryland, July 9, 1830. He was educated in the common schools of Fayette County, Pennsylvania, and studied medicine under, among others, his cousin, Dr. James Porter of Frostburg (*see* note 145 above). G. Ellis Porter took his medical diploma from Jefferson Medical College, Philadelphia, in 1853. In 1861, he was practicing in Lonaconing, and there took an active and vocal part in raising troops for the Union. He was mustered in as major of the Second Regiment Potomac Home Brigade in August 28, 1861, and promoted to lieutenant colonel January 3, 1862. Porter commanded the regiment from December 1863 to its mustering out October 2, 1864. That same month he took charge of the military hospital at Cumberland and remained in that post until the end of the war. After the war, he returned to his thriving practice in Lonaconing, published professional papers and served actively in local and state professional societies. J. Scharf, *History of Western Maryland*, vol. 2, pp. 1504; Wilmer, *History and Roster of Maryland Volunteers*, vol. 1, p. 543.

[147] Dr. Samuel P. Smith (1795-still alive as of 1888) served as surgeon of the Second Maryland Home Brigade from August 1861 to October 4, 1864. A native of Frederick, Maryland, Smith served as a militia infantryman in the war of 1812 (witnessing the bombardment of Fort McHenry). He studied medicine under local physicians and at Maryland University Hospital in Baltimore, from which he was graduated in 1817. He established a practice in Cumberland in 1820 and quickly rose to local prominence. He served three terms as a Whig in the state legislature, was a member of the constitutional convention of 1851, was a director of the Chesapeake and Ohio Canal and of the Second National Bank of Cumberland. On August 27, 1861, he was mustered in as surgeon of the Second Regiment Potomac Home Brigade and served in that capacity until mustered out October 4, 1864. Dr. Smith was venerated in his community and the surrounding coal regions. Scharf, *History of Western Maryland*, vol. 2, pp. 1403; Wilmer, *History and Roster of Maryland Volunteers*, vol. 1, p. 543.

[148] Benjamin Franklin Kelley (1807-1891), Union general, commanded the Railroad District, Middle Department, to September 1862 and the defenses of the Upper Potomac, Eighth Corps, Middle Department, in January and February 1863.

[149] "Riff raff" is a slang term for disreputable people. Roy, or perhaps the typesetter, erred and most likely meant to use "rip raps" which was a common term for stone jetties or foundations around harbors. Military prisoners were often set to hard labor on rip raps.

[150] Roy later wrote that "several of the pieces [were] nearly a [sic] inch square." Roy to J. L. Davenport, Commissioner of Pensions, April 27, 1910, Roy Pension File, National Archives, Washington, D.C.

[151] In 1862, the U.S. government paid its private soldiers thirteen dollars per month, so ten dollars represented about three weeks pay for Roy.

[152] If Roy first visited Dr. Smith in Baltimore in the early summer of 1863, as he suggests at the end of Chapter 16, then his second visit to Baltimore must have occurred in August or September 1863, after his discharge from the army in June 1863.

[153] The text reads: "quisically."

Chapter 18 — Another Surgical Operation

[154] George Bean was mustered into Company F, Tenth Pennsylvania Reserve Volunteer Corps (Thirty-ninth Pennsylvania Volunteer Infantry) June 19, 1861, and discharged October 30, 1862, for wounds received at Gaines's Mill. Bates, *History of Pennsylvania Volunteers*, vol. 1, p. 834.

[155] Dr. Albert Gustav Walter (1811-1876), was born in Germany and educated at Königsberg University. After a year of postgraduate work in Berlin, he began a journey to America. A storm wrecked the ship off the coast of Norway, and Walter lost everything but the clothing he wore. He worked as a law clerk in London for a year while furthering his medical studies under a local physician. He again tried passage to America, and in 1835 was working in Nashville, Tennessee, where his patients included injured or crippled slaves. He became an outspoken critic of slavery, and moved to Pittsburgh in 1837. He opened a practice, married, and in the 1850s built a private hospital (Walter's Surgical Hospital, a two-story brick structure, stood at Cooper and Bluff Streets, which is now on the campus of Duquesne University). He specialized in corrective surgery and the rehabilitation of industrial injuries and is considered a surgical pioneer. He performed in 1858 the first operation successful in repairing a ruptured bladder. Dr. Walter wrote extensively on his findings and earned an international reputation for his work. He died of pneumonia. George Swetnam, "Hospital of History," The Pittsburgh *Press*, November 3, 1968, pp. 4-5 (See biographical files in Pennsylvania Room, Carnegie Library, Pittsburgh). *Bulletin of the Allegheny County Medical Society*, November 7, 1959, p. 859. *Who Was Who in America*, Historical Volume, 1607-1896, (Chicago, 1967), p. 631. See also *Directory of Pittsburgh and Allegheny Cities, the Adjoining Boroughs and Villages for 1863-1864* (Pittsburgh, 1863), pp. 347-348.

[156] In 1910, Roy wrote that Walter, "cut me on both sides of the wound, and put his middle finger in of each hand until they met; he then extracted two pieces with his forceps." Roy to J. L. Davenport, Commissioner of Pensions, April 27, 1910, Roy Pension File, National Archives, Washington, D.C.

[157] James Abram Garfield (1831-1881), Union general and twentieth president of the United States, was assassinated July 2, 1881, and died two and a half months later.

[158] If Dr. Walter operated on Roy in the autumn of 1863, as the sequence of events suggests, Roy was no longer a private in the Union army. Roy was discharged June

13, 1863 (see Afterword). Perhaps he wore his uniform because he had no other suitable clothing or perhaps because he understood that soldiers sometimes benefited from special treatment by patriotic citizens.

[159] The chronology of events suggests that Roy's sudden improvement occurred in October or November 1863. A month or so later, he met Janet Watson at Joseph Stewart's wedding.

[160] Roy was discharged in the summer of 1863, *before* he got well. He underwent the second operation by Dr. Smith and the operations by Dr. Walter in the autumn of that year, after his release from the army.

[161] Roy ends his tale on a note of gratitude and satisfaction: "The soldiers of the War of the Rebellion have been liberally cared for by the government, which their valor saved from being overthrown by the mad passion of the Southern slave holding oligarchy. The preservation of the Union cost many hundred million dollars and many hundred thousand lives; but the cost in men and money was none too great in view of the results. The soldiers of the Union Army have bequeathed to their descendants, a rich inheritance, for which they will be honored by a grateful country as long as civilized man inhabits the earth."

Afterword

[162] Roy deposed in 1906 that fourteen pieces of bone had been taken from his wound, but states in his memoir (*see* chapter 17) that Dr. Smith in Baltimore alone removed fourteen pieces. In 1910, Roy stated Dr. Smith had taken out sixteen fragments. Since other surgeons extracted bone fragments as well, it would seem the total number would be higher than fourteen but perhaps not as high as fifty. It is difficult to reconcile Roy's statements about how much bone had been removed, unless the first examining surgeon misunderstood the patient to say "upwards of fifty pieces" when Roy might have said "upwards of fifteen pieces." Roy to J. L. Davenport, Commissioner of Pensions, April 27, 1910, Roy Pension File, National Archives, Washington, D. C.

[163] Roy to J. L. Davenport, April 27, 1910, Roy Pension File, National Archives, Washington, D.C.

[164] J. Richards deposition, August 12, 1912, Roy Pension File, National Archives, Washington, D.C.

[165] Dr. D. B. Warren deposition, April 23, 1913, Roy Pension File, National Archives, Washington, D.C.

[166] Janet Roy died August 22, 1928. Roy Pension File, National Archives, Washington, D.C.

[167] Obituary notice in The Jackson (Ohio) *Herald*, October 20-21, 1914.

[168] Roy to J. L. Davenport, April 27, 1910, Roy Pension File, National Archives, Washington, D. C.

Appendix 2

[169] Brigadier General George A. McCall. Brigadier General John F. Reynolds. Brigadier General George G. Meade. Brigadier General E. O. C. Ord.

[170] The arrival of some of the Pennsylvania Reserves in Washington following the stunning Federal defeat at the First Battle of Bull Run did not literally save the

capital from capture or even assault. The Confederates in command at Manassas decided immediately after the battle ended on July 21 that pursuit of the defeated Northerners was impractical, and their decision was in no way influenced by the imminent arrive of Federal troops in Washington. The arrival of the Reserves did, however, do much to shore up the flagging spirits of many in the capital city and certainly did boost the confidence of those who believed the Confederates would soon make an attempt to capture the city. The Southerners were content to hold the ground they had captured at Bull Run.

[171] Roy is nearly correct in his figures, at least according to reports in the *Official Records of the Union and Confederate Armies*. The Pennsylvania Reserves took, by the "liberal estimate" of their commander, General George Gordon Meade, 4,500 men into the attack at Fredericksburg on December 13, 1862. Meade reported 175 men killed, 1,241 wounded and 437 captured or missing — a total of 1,853, or 20 fewer than Roy's total (Roy, or the typesetter, added 20 to the captured or missing figure). General George Pickett reported 232 killed, 1,157 wounded and 1,499 captured or missing for a total of 2,888 casualties in his division's famous charge on July 3, 1863, at Gettysburg. Pickett began the assault with roughly 4,900 men, considerably fewer than Roy's figure of 6,204. These figures yield total casualty percentages of 41.1 percent for the Reserves at Fredericksburg and 58.9 for Pickett at Gettysburg. *OR*, I, 21, pp. 140, 512; Ibid, I, 27, pt. 2, p. 339; Edwin B. Coddington, *The Gettysburg Campaign: A Study in Command* (New York, 1968), p. 803, n. 173.

Appendix 3 — Union Sentiment in the South

[172] Roy refers to the remark attributed to Lincoln in December 1863 by his personal secretary John Hay. "The President last night had a dream. He was in a party of plain people and as it became known who he was they began to comment on his appearance. One of them said, 'He is a common-looking man.' The President replied, 'Common-looking people are the best in the world: that is the reason the Lord makes so many of them.'" *Letters of John Hay and Extracts from his Diary*, C. L. Hay, ed.

[173] The accepted modern form is "Arkansans."

[174] The text reads "anti-bellum."

[175] Roy refers to William Meade Fishback (1831-1903), a native Virginian and prewar business acquaintance of Abraham Lincoln who settled in Fort Smith, Arkansas, in 1858. Attorney Fishback freely professed his opposition to secession and voters sent his pro-Union voice to the state convention called to consider secession. Fishback apparently reversed his stand after the firing of Fort Sumter and went so far as to declare that any use of force by the Federal government to coerce states from disunion should be resisted "to the last extremity." As Roy suggests, however, this about face might itself have been due to coercion, for in mid-1862, Fishback moved to Missouri and took the oath of allegiance to the United States. He returned to Arkansas the next year to raise a regiment of Unionists, but failed, so Roy is mistaken in believing the "Colonel" fought for the Union at the head of troops. Roy is mistaken as well about the year in which Fishback became Arkansas's chief executive. Fishback was reelected to the state

legislature in 1884 (his third term) and did not become governor until 1892. *Dictionary of American Biography*, vol. 6, p. 403.

Appendix 4 — Roy's Winter on the Rio Grande

[176] Roy probably means Laredo, Texas, on the Rio Grande.

Index

A

abductor lurch (Trendelenburg gait)   103
Abolitionists   115, 135
Acquia Creek, Virginia   68
Adams, Joseph A.   128
Adams, Milo Romulus   126, 127, 144
ambulance   99
anesthesia   102, 129
Annapolis, Maryland   69, 70, 73–77, 142
antibiotics   105
Army of Northern Virginia   91
Army of the Potomac   60–62, 65, 75, 108, 120
Arouet, Francois-Marie. *See* Voltaire
arthritis   103
Austerlitz, battle of   59, 139

B

bacteriology   10, 100, 106
Baltimore & Ohio Railroad   78, 88, 89, 145
Baltimore, Maryland   73, 148
Bannockburn, battle of   72, 143
Barragh, Thomas L.   126
Bates, John Coalter   139
Bean, George   88, 149
Beaver Dam Creek, battle of   16–19, 124, 125, 140
Bedford, Pennsylvania   78
Belle Isle Prison   45, 46, 54, 134
Boatswain's Creek   19
Bonaparte, Charles Louis Napoleon   129
Bradford, Augustus Williamson   144
Bruce, King Robert   57, 72

Bryant, William Cullen   43, 79, 133
Buchanan, James   78
Buckley, W. W.   125
Bull Run, battles of   16, 33, 46, 58, 68, 72, 108, 120, 143
Burns, Robert   14, 42, 43, 54, 57, 79, 81, 133
Butler, Benjamin Franklin   120
Butler County, Pennsylvania   124
Byron, Lord (George Gordon)   14, 42, 43, 56, 133, 138

C

C.S.S. Virginia   141
Cameron, James   143
Cameron, John   72, 120
Cameron, Simon   120, 143
Camp Parole   69, 70, 71, 77, 143
Campbell, Robert   50, 136
camphor in oil   131
Castle Thunder   135
causalgia   103
Chaffee, Adna Romanza   138
Chandler, Harrison J.   126
"Change of Base"   133
Chesapeake and Ohio Canal   145, 148
Chesapeake General Hospital   142
Chickahominy River   13, 16–19, 24, 27, 31, 39, 60, 61, 134
Childe Harold's Pilgrimage   79, 138
chloroform   129
Churchill, Ohio   93
City Point, Virginia   64, 141
Civil War
    beginnings of   14, 31, 114–115
    combatant relations   17, 29, 31–32, 112
    medicine   10, 23, 29

morale of troops   39, 66, 75
mortality rate   9
newspaper accounts of   45, 52, 69
societal effects of   9, 10
treatment of prisoners   55
treatment of wounded   27–30, 35–37, 51, 71
Clarysville General Hospital   71, 75, 77, 79, 83, 91, 145, 146
Cole, Rufus D.   126
Commodore   64, 69, 141
Constitution of the United States   31, 66
"Copperheads"   147
Crawford, Samuel   136
Crockett, James   111
Cromwell, Oliver   129
Cumberland, Maryland   80, 147, 148
Curtin, Andrew Gregg   16

D

Dante Alighieri   47, 135
Davis, Jefferson   39, 53, 64, 132, 133
debridement   105
Declaration of Independence   117
DeHart, Henry V.   124
Desdemona   146
Divine Comedy, The   135
Douglas, Stephen A.   114
doxology   64
Dranesville, Virginia   124
Duquesne University   149

E

Early, Jubal A.   140, 145
Eckhart Mines, Maryland   79, 147
Edward II, king of England   143
Ellerson's Mill, Virginia   17
Ellis, William   147

F

Fair Oaks, battle of   144
Falmouth, Virginia   16, 77, 124
fire-eaters   118
Fishback, William Meade   151, 152
Fort McHenry, Maryland   148
Fort Monroe, Virginia   143
Fort Smith, Arkansas   111
Fort Sumter, South Carolina   14, 110
Frederick, Maryland   148
Frederick the Great   138
Fredericksburg, battle of   77, 109, 145
Free Soil Democrats   115
Frostburg, Maryland   13, 14, 75, 77, 84, 92, 147, 148

G

Gaines's Mill, battle of   10, 19–24, 27, 33, 38, 45, 59, 62, 69, 77, 92, 112, 140
Gaines's Mill, Virginia   17–21, 44, 49
Galesburg, Illinois   121
Galileo   111
Garfield, James Abram   88, 149
Garrison, William Lloyd   31, 130
General Hospital. *See* Clarysville General Hospital
General Hospital at Cumberland, Maryland   146
George's Creek   89
Gettysburg, battle of   108
Gettysburg, Pennsylvania   91
Glasgow, Scotland   125
Glen Roy Cemetery   95
Glen Roy, Ohio   94-95
Glendale, battle of   33, 127, 144
Goldsmith, Oliver   131, 142
Grant, Ulysses S.   59–60, 139
Greeley, Horace   31, 111, 130

H

Halleck, Henry Wager   68, 142
hardtack   132
Harrison's Landing   64, 68, 141
Hawley, Thomas   33, 130
Healey, T. A.   147
Higginbotham, Edward
    Garrigues   135, 140
Hill, A. P.   19
hope   101
hypotension   100

I

ilium   98
infection   98, 105
intestines   98
intravenous fluids   104
Irish Brigade   126

J

Jackson, C. Feger   125
Jackson, Thomas J. "Stone-
    wall"   17, 27, 28, 29, 31, 38,
    60, 129, 132
James River   45, 61
Jefferson Medical College, Philadel-
    phia   148
Jefferson, Thomas   118
Johnson, Samuel   75, 144

K

Kelley, Benjamin Franklin   85, 148
Kirk, James T.   125
Knox College   115

L

Laredo, Texas   152
"laudable pus"   100
Lee, Robert E.   9, 17–19, 59–61,
    70, 91, 130, 132
Lewis, J. B.   79, 83, 91, 102, 146
Libby Prison   27, 45, 48–63, 67,
    71, 135, 136, 137, 140
lice   137

limp   99, 103
Lincoln, Abraham   14, 43, 60, 83,
    110, 114–121, 139, 151
liquor (medicinal)   99
Litchfield, Connecticut   75
Longfellow, Henry Wadsworth   43,
    79, 133
Lowry, M. C.   25, 32, 35, 40, 49–
    51, 56, 59, 60, 69, 70, 71, 77,
    128

M

Maclaren, Ian   84, 147
maggots   100, 130
Magruder, John Bankhead   134
Manassas, Virginia   16
Mansfield   120
Maryland Infantry
    Second Regiment Potomac Home
        Brigade   78, 81, 145, 148
Maryland University Hospital   148
Massachusetts Infantry
    Fifth Regiment   144
    Tenth Regiment   143
McCall, George A.   16, 108, 150
McClellan, George B.   16–19, 24,
    25, 38, 45, 59–62, 66–68, 69,
    75, 120, 139, 141, 142
McClellan's Own Story   61
McCracken, George W.   127
McDowell, Irvin   124
McKee, James   126
McKinney, David   99, 125
McMillan, Hugh   33, 130
Meade, George Gordon   60, 108,
    139, 150
Meagher, Thomas   23
Mechanicsville, battle of. *See* Beaver
    Dam Creek, battle of
medication   100
Miles, Nelson Appleton   138
Milton, John   14, 42, 49, 57, 133
Minera, Texas   112

Missouri Compromise   114, 117
Moorberger, James M.   126

N

Napoleon   56, 57, 61, 129, 139
Naval Academy. *See* U.S. Naval
    Academy
nerve damage   98, 103
New York Highlanders   72
New York Infantry
    Fifth Regiment   126
    Ninety-fourth Regiment   128
    Second Regiment   143
    Seventy-ninth Regiment 71-72,
        120, 143
Norvall, James   143

O

Ohio River   117
Ohr, C. H.   92
Olcott, William   126
Ord, E. O. C.   108
osteomyelitis   98, 101
Othello   80, 146

P

pain   102
Paradise Lost   42, 49, 79, 133, 136
Pennsylvania Central Railroad   78
Pennsylvania Reserve Corps   16–
    19, 32, 51, 66, 91, 108–109,
    151
    Eighth Regiment   132
    Eleventh Regiment   127
    Ninth Regiment   19, 125
    Second Regiment   126
    Tenth Regiment   16, 124, 145,
        149
    Thirteenth Regiment   136
Petersburg, Virginia   64
Phillips, Wendell   111
Pickett, George   151
Pickett's division   109
Pittsburgh, Pennsylvania   87, 124

Pope, John   68, 70, 142
Porter, Fitz John   16, 27, 61
Porter, G. Ellis   84–85, 148
Porter, James   84, 85, 89, 147, 148
Potomac River   91
prisoners of war
    exchange of, parole of   142

Q

Queen City Hotel, Cumberland,
    Maryland   80

R

Rachel   133
Rappahannock River   16, 77
Regular U.S. Army   126
Reynolds, John F.   108, 150
Rhode Island Light Artillery, Battery
    C (Weeden's)   125
Richmond & York Railroad   44,
    134
Richmond, Virginia   13, 24, 44–
    47, 57, 61, 68
Robert de Bruce   138, 143
Rohrer, Benjamin   125
Roy, Andrew
    children of   93, 94, 95
    death of   95
    early life of   13–14
        emigration to Maryland   13
        family of   13
        Scottish heritage   13
        self-education of   14
        settles in Arkansas   14, 42,
            110
    employment of   14, 42, 92, 93,
        94, 112
    love of literature   75
    marriage of   81
    memoir of   9–12, 94
    military service of
        as prisoner of war   44–47
        enlistment   14–16, 81

medical discharge of 91
opinion of McClellan 60–62
paroled from Libby
   Prison 63–65
receives pension 92
sees first combat 16–19
training 16
transferred to Camp Parole 71
transferred to Fortress
   Monroe 69–71
transferred to General Hospital 72
transferred to General Hospital,
   Clarysville 78–83
political views of 14, 57, 110
wounding of
   description of wound 97–99
   effect of over-exertion 64
   effect of spirit of survival 70
   first Confederate surgeon's
      inspection 29
   incurs wound 21
   initial field treatment 23–26,
      99–100
   initial infection and ver-
      min 35–37, 39, 100
   modern perspective on 104–
      106
   results of wound later in
      life 103–104
   self-treatment in field 38–41,
      100
   self-treatment in Libby
      Prison 52, 54–55, 100
   surgeon's exam at Camp Pa-
      role 101
   surgeon's exam at Camp Pa-
      role 71–72
   surgeon's exam at Naval Acad-
      emy Hospital 76, 101
   surgeon's exam at Naval Acad-
      emy Hospital 73–74

surgery upon by Dr.
   Smith 85–86, 102
surgery upon by Dr.
   Walter 87–89, 102
treatment at Clarysville General
   Hospital 79–80, 101–102
treatment at Fortress Monroe 70–71, 101
treatment at mother's
   home 79
vermin 54
Roy, Augustus 74–75, 144
Roy, David Tod (son) 95
Roy, James (son) 94
Roy, Janet Watson (wife) 80–81,
   90, 93, 150
Roy, Maggie (daughter) 93
Roy, Mrs. David (mother) 69, 70,
   79

S

Satan 133
Savage's Station 24, 44–46, 132,
   135
Savage's Station, battle of 45
Sayers, Robert A. 40–41, 49, 51,
   132
Schell, H. S. 128, 130
Seven Days' Fight 24, 45, 60, 61–
   62, 74
Seven Pines, battle of. See Fair Oaks,
   battle of
Seward, William H. 120
Shakespeare, William 14, 42, 43,
   50, 57, 79, 81, 126, 131, 132,
   146
Sheridan, Philip H. 60, 139
Sherman, William Tecumseh 37,
   60, 131, 139
shock 99
simplex cerrate 129
Skelton, James A. 127
Sloan, Alexander 80

Smith, Nathan Ryno   84–86, 87–88, 102, 147, 149, 150
Smith, Samuel P.   84, 147, 148
Somerset County, Pennsylvania   124
Spier, Andrew   78–79, 81, 85, 145
Spotsylvania   60
Stanhope, fourth earl of   130
Stentor   64
Sterne, Laurence   129
Stewart, Ephriam P.   126
Stewart, Joseph   23, 80, 125, 146, 150
Sumner, Charles   31, 130
Sykes, George   126, 129

T

Tam O'Shanter   133
Townsend, M. M.   79–80, 83, 86, 101, 144, 146
Tragedy of King Lear, The   131
Tragedy of Macbeth, The   126
Tragedy of Othello, the Moor of Venice, The   146
Turner, Richard R.   138
Turner, Thomas Pratt   137
turpentine   100, 131

U

U.S. Artillery Fifth, Battery C (DeHart's)   124
U.S. Military Academy   24
U.S. Naval Academy   73, 143
U.S. Naval Academy General Hospital. See Clarysville General Hospital
U.S. Naval Academy Hospital   69, 71
U.S. Sanitary Commission   141
U.S.S. Galena   131
U.S.S. Monitor   64, 141
University of Maryland Medical School   147

V

Vale Summit, Maryland   79, 80, 81, 84, 125, 146
Vogelweide, Walther von der   138
Voltaire   138

W

Wallace, Sir William   57, 138
Walter, Albert Gustav   87–90, 102, 149
Washington, George   118, 121
Waters, W. E.   128
Watson, Janet   146, 150. See Roy, Janet Watson
Watson, John. See Maclaren, Ian
Weeden, William B.   125
Wellston, Ohio   94
Wellsville, West Virginia   87
West Point. See U.S. Military Academy
Wheeling, West Virginia   88, 89
Whigs   115
Whittier, John Greenleaf   43, 133
Winder, John   137
Woodward, Evan   126
wounded
    rations for   130
    treatment of   131, 132
wounds
    general discussion of   97
    irrigation of   101

X

X-ray   100, 104

Y

Young, Samuel Baldwin Marks   138

Z

Zouaves   126

About the Editor

William J. Miller is editor of *Civil War* magazine and author or editor of six books on the Civil War. His *Mapping for Stonewall: The Civil War Service of Jed Hotchkiss* won the Fletcher Pratt Award as the best Civil War book of 1993. He lives in Virginia's Shenandoah Valley.

About the Medical Commentator

Clyde B. Kernek, M.D., author of *Field Surgeon at Gettysburg*, is associate professor of orthopædic surgery at Indiana University School of Medicine. He served overseas in the U.S. Army Medical Corps treating soldiers with war wounds from 1968–71.